Going Home An

Going Home Another Way

Daily readings and resources for Christmastide

Neil Paynter

WILD GOOSE PUBLICATIONS

www.ionabooks.com

Contents of book © the individual contributors
Compilation © 2008 Neil Paynter

First published 2008 by
Wild Goose Publications,
4th Floor, Savoy House, 140 Sauchiehall St, Glasgow G2 3DH, UK.
Wild Goose Publications is the publishing division of the Iona Community.
Scottish Charity No. SCO03794. Limited Company Reg. No. SCO96243.
www.ionabooks.com

ISBN 978-1-905010-57-8

Cover photo © Sacred Destinations (www.sacred-destinations.com)
Used by permission.
Carving from Autun Cathedral, Burgundy, made by the 12th-century sculptor Gislebertus.

The publishers gratefully acknowledge the support of the Drummond Trust,
3 Pitt Terrace, Stirling FK8 2EY in producing this book.

Overseas distribution:
Australia: Willow Connection Pty Ltd, Unit 4A, 3-9 Kenneth Road,
Manly Vale, NSW 2093
New Zealand: Pleroma, Higginson Street, Otane 4170, Central Hawkes Bay
Canada: Novalis/Bayard Publishing & Distribution, 10 Lower Spadina Ave.,
Suite 400, Toronto, Ontario M5V 2Z2

Printed by Bell & Bain, Thornliebank, Glasgow

Contents

Follow truth wherever you find it. Even if it takes you outside your preconceived ideas of God or life. Even if it takes you outside your own country into most insignificant alien places like Bethlehem. Be courageous. But concentrate on your search. Truth is one. All roads lead to Home. The seeming devious route will take you to a single star. You will find it is the morning star for you. In the end you will see the Sun behind all suns (as the Celts called Jesus Christ).

And be courageous. Jesus is no static figure. He is the Living Water that follows you through the parched desert. His constancy is in His movement. In the end, moving from the particular, you will find the truth of the general. And you will give Him preeminence in all things material, and in all things spiritual – gold and incense. And you will be prepared to die with Him.

Ultimate truth is in Jesus Christ, the Light of the World and its Life.

George MacLeod, 1958

Introduction

Iona was a great place to be at Christmastime and New Year. I remember walking to the north beach on Christmas Eve to shop for Christmas gifts – stones, seashells, feathers; making a candle in the craft room for a guest from America; bread sauce, and the smell of cloves from the kitchen – and the most beautiful Christmas tree I have ever seen in my life: a tree decorated not with the glitz and clutter of baubles, tinsel and lights, but with real, red apples … Shiny. Curved and delicious as God's good world …

I remember New Year's Eve: the crackle and sizzle of fireworks raining down like jewellery; dancing Strip the Willow in the village hall and waking up with bruises; dancing to *Back in the USSR* by the Beatles and *Auld Lang Syne* by Eddi Reader – holding hands in a big circle; single malt whisky with neighbours in the village, and – on the way home – the path of the moon across the great restless sea.

And after Christmas, in the dark days, when everything seemed over, closed up, buried, asleep, the solidarity, encouragement and companionship of community. The discipline and rhythm of work and worship. I missed that most when I left the island. That is one reason why I put this book together. On the mainland there were years when I lost the heart to travel into the New Year with faith and hope. Years when I couldn't read, or even see, the stars … got lost on the way. There were times when I felt so swamped by commercialism and propaganda I found it near impossible to hear God's Word; and times when I found it hard to glimpse or grasp anything sacred in the secular.

May this little book be a friend through the joy and euphoria of Christmas and New Year, but also give you strength, inspiration – feed you, companion you, challenge you – in the in-between times. There are good-hearted, human companions here. And we all need good companions as we journey through this cold, hard, bewildering, amazing, gorgeous world; this gift of a life.

At this time of year, I always remember, and hold on to, these words from George MacLeod: *Follow the light you have and pray for more light.*

Neil Paynter

A watch night service

John Harvey

The service starts at about 11:30pm, and can be preceded by carol singing, preferably outside, round the parish. When the worshippers enter the church, the lighting should be quite low, if possible, and each person should be given a lighted candle in a candle-holder and a copy of the order of service, with the songs printed out in full.

Welcome and introduction

Opening responses

Men and women, why are you here?
WE ARE HERE TO WAIT AND TO WATCH.

Men and women, for what do you wait?
WE WAIT FOR NEW HOPE, AND NEW LIFE.

Men and women, for whom do you watch?
WE WATCH FOR THE LIGHT THAT NO DARKNESS CAN PUT OUT.

Men and women, how would you wait and watch?
WE WOULD WATCH AND WAIT WITH ALL OUR HEART,
WITH ALL OUR SOUL
AND WITH ALL OUR MIGHT.

Song: 'When Out of Poverty Is Born' (CH4* 291)

Prayer

God beyond naming,
God beyond defining,
God for whom we yearn,
God we want to trust,
    hear our prayer.
We are not many wise,
not many great,
not many powerful,
    but we dare to ask
    for a word from you
    this night.
We have looked for you
in many ways and places,
in desperate trouble,
in deep despair,
when all else fails,
to come with might and power.
    Tonight, we would look for you
    in a different way,
    and in a different place.
In tenderness and in pain,
in quietness and in secret,
in human need and parents' love,
in joy, but also in suffering.
    Show us yourself
    in the baby of Bethlehem

> and help us to see you
> as you really are.
> We pray in the name of that same child,
> Jesus, Mary's Son. Amen

Reading: St Luke 1:26–38

Read by three people, if possible, one reading as the narrator, one as the angel and one as Mary.

Reflection: on the theme of waiting and watching

Someone who has been recently, or is currently, pregnant could speak briefly about her thoughts and feelings at this time. The person leading the service could then speak, equally briefly, about common human hopes and expectations – relating them to today, to the experience of the congregation and to her/his own hopes and expectations.

A short period of silence, for people to do their own reflecting on what has been said and sung so far.

Song: 'God's Surprise' (*Heaven Shall Not Wait: Wild Goose Songs, Volume One;* tune: Scarlet Ribbons)

Towards the end of this song, the lights of the church are gradually dimmed, until only the candles are left lit.

Prayer at midnight

Wonderful God,
at the beginning of everything,
you said: 'Let there be light'
and there was light and life in all the earth.

And when men and women had grown tired,
weary of the darkness
of anxiety, confusion and sin,
you came into that darkness,
in Jesus, the true light
who lightens everyone born into our world.
Once again it is dark –
not just dark at midnight
but dark within and among us:
the darkness of doubt and fearfulness,
of warfare and hunger and illness,
the darkness of conflicting voices,
the darkness of death.

Once again, we welcome you
bending so low to creep in among us,
not forcing, not shouting,
too gentle to even flicker our candle flames.
Make your home among us again, we pray;
be our guest, in heart and home and city,
in the empty, howling wastelands of our times,
and light up our world once again
with the new hope

and the new life
that faith in you still brings.
We pray in Jesus's name, and for his sake. Amen

When this prayer ends, the lights of the church are turned fully up, people are invited to blow out their candles, and to greet their neighbours with a Christmas Day greeting. As the greetings end, a solo voice could be singing, for example, 'The Aye Carol' (Heaven Shall Not Wait).

Song: 'Make Way!' (CH4 279)

Closing responses

The desert will sing and shout for joy;
EVERYONE WILL SEE THE LORD'S SPLENDOUR,
SEE GOD'S GREATNESS AND POWER.

Tell everyone who is discouraged:
'BE STRONG AND DON'T BE AFRAID!'

The blind will be able to see,
THE DEAF WILL BE ABLE TO HEAR.

The lame will leap and dance,
THOSE WHO CAN'T SPEAK WILL SHOUT FOR JOY.

This is the promise of God.
GOD'S PROMISE WILL BE FULFILLED.

Benediction

We go out into Christmas Day
in the peace of Jesus Christ.
May his peace,
which lightens the soul with faith,
lifts the spirit with hope
and leavens the world with love,
be yours tonight and always.
And the blessing of God –
Creator, Son and Spirit –
go with you, and stay with you,
now and always.
AMEN

CH4 – Church Hymnary 4, John L. Bell (ed.), Canterbury Press

Christmas Day

Kathy Galloway

Bible readings

The people who walked in darkness have seen a great light; those who lived in a land of deep darkness – on them light has shined. You have multiplied the nation, you have increased its joy; they rejoice before you as with joy at the harvest, as people exult when dividing plunder. For the yoke of their burden, and the bar across their shoulders, the rod of their oppressor, you have broken as on the day of Midian. For all the boots of the tramping warriors and all the garments rolled in blood shall be burned as fuel for the fire. For a child has been born for us, a son given to us; authority rests upon his shoulders; and he is named Wonderful Counselor, Mighty God, Everlasting Father, Prince of Peace. His authority shall grow continually, and there shall be endless peace for the throne of David and his kingdom. He will establish and uphold it with justice and with righteousness from this time onward and forevermore. The zeal of the Lord of hosts will do this.

Isaiah 9:2–7 (NRSV)

In those days a decree went out from Emperor Augustus that all the world should be registered. This was the first registration and was taken while Quirinius was governor of Syria. All went to their own towns to be registered. Joseph also went from the town of Nazareth in Galilee to Judea, to the city of David called Bethlehem, because he was descended from the house and family of David. He went to be registered with Mary, to whom he was engaged and who was expecting a child. While they were there, the time came for her to deliver her child. And she gave birth to her firstborn son and wrapped him in bands of cloth, and laid him in a manger, because there was no place for them in the inn.

In that region there were shepherds living in the fields, keeping watch over their flock by night. Then an angel of the Lord stood before them, and the glory of the Lord shone around them, and they were terrified. But the angel said to them, 'Do not be afraid; for see – I am bringing you good news of great joy for all the people: to you is

born this day in the city of David a Saviour, who is the Messiah, the Lord. This will be a
sign for you: you will find a child wrapped in bands of cloth and lying in a manger.'
And suddenly there was with the angel a multitude of the heavenly host, praising God
and saying,

> 'Glory to God in the highest heaven,
> and on earth peace among those whom he favours!'

Luke 2:1–14 (NRSV)

Reflection

A few years ago, I read an extraordinary little piece about Christmas in the news-
paper. It described how Richard Lewis, the Bishop of St Edmundsbury and
Ipswich, had 'startled his flock by insisting that the Christmas message should
include secret police, the massacre of children by troops and contemplation of
the baby Jesus as a refugee and asylum seeker'. Since the biblical texts do, of
course, describe exactly these facts, there's no 'should' about it, and if the good
Christians of the Bishop's flock were startled by any of this, it does make you
wonder exactly what Bible they had been reading. But I suspect the startled
person was really the reporter!

It is precisely because of their contemporary resonances that the Christmas
scriptures make for uncomfortable, even ambivalent listening. How shall we hear
Isaiah 9, speaking of dividing captured wealth, of defeated nations, of lifting the
burden of oppression and exploitation, how shall we imagine the boots of the
invading army and their bloodstained clothing? How shall America hear Isaiah 9,
and Iraq and Afghanistan, and how shall they read of censuses and mangers in
Bethlehem, Bethlehem of the tanks and barbed wire, Bethlehem under occupation now as it was then. Our sacred scriptures are not simple or safe or capable of
only one interpretation, only one truth. They are complex and dangerous and full

of different, sometimes opposite meanings, and people have a habit of finding in them the truth that suits their own interests.

But why should they not be so? Indeed, it's good that they are. Because human life, including our lives, is not simple or safe or containing only one meaning. Life, our lives, are complex and dangerous and we negotiate our way all the time through different truths, and hear the same story told from a thousand viewpoints. What is the truth, for example, about our Christmas celebration? That it has become an over-commercialised feast of consumer consumption, far removed from the true spirit of Christmas? But I like to send greetings to friends, especially those I don't see often, at least once in the year. And I like to give gifts to those I love, and feel it is in the true spirit of Christmas to do that.

> *Voices raised in ancient songs, praising, telling of joy and sounding odd beside*
>   *the current rage,*
> *In this turmoil, a moment of calm, and to behold it, come all the faithful, all of*
>   *the faithful.*
> *They gather now to sing Hallelujah for everyone to hear –*
> *Oh, but the rest of the year!*[1]

The truth about celebrating Christmas? My truth is that I have competing and conflicting feelings about it – guilt about my complicity in injustice, passionate sorrow for those whose Christmas will be spent lonely or bereft, or sick or anxious, in prison or in exile or in danger or on a battlefield or under bombing, rage for those whose lives have been violently ended. Yet also gratitude for the care and generosity it brings out in so many, respect for the courage of people who refuse to let adverse circumstances destroy the human instinct to feast and be joyful, sheer wonder at the fact that the dream and the hope of a more just and loving world refuses to die in spite of all the evidence to the contrary, that the star still leads us on.

And so, as I struggle with the complexity of life, as I seek to find meaning and hope and justice in a dangerous world, I am glad that the star leads to Bethlehem; not a sanitised Middle Eastern Brigadoon that appears once a year out of a sentimental mist, but the Bethlehem where a baby is being born into great danger in a shed in a country under military occupation. I am glad to remember imperfect families and extravagant and inappropriate gifts, hard journeys and strange relationships, mysterious messages and life-changing meetings. I am glad to remember sick children and soldiers and hard-won friendships, swindlers and crooks and adulterers and a whole host of compromised human beings. I am glad to celebrate this birth with those I love.

Above all, I am glad that the birth of a baby in Bethlehem is a sign, not of retreat into Christmas Disneyland, some half-baked, dangerous fantasy of perfection and virtue, but of the life of God placed in human hands, not escaping from history but entering into it. There is no hope for any of us, nor peace nor real love, in Christmas Disneyland, or in any of its multi-faith varieties. What we get is a baby born into a dangerous and impoverished world. Not a miracle, just a baby. One, moreover, who had to flee as a refugee from the swords of war, whose life and teaching led him into conflict, and who ended up dying violently and ignominiously. Peace didn't break out the day he was born either!

The word of life and hope and love made flesh in Jesus speaks in and through all our compromised realities, all our frailties, all our failures, all the difficulties and complexities of life. If it does not speak in these, and if we do not speak it to these, then it does not speak at all. But I believe that the word speaks, in Bethlehem and Baghdad and Washington DC and Glasgow. It says, 'you are a human being. You are loved and precious.' It says, 'we must be human.' It says 'Glory to God in the highest. God is good.'

The soles of his feet have touched the earth. All hail, let there be joy!

Christmas Day
Angels and stars,
shepherds and travellers,
a newborn child

An old story
full of love and danger,
laying bare the beauty
of an amazing God.[2]

The blessing of God with us now
and peace to the world
Amen

December 26th

Peter Millar

Bible reading

As the members of the Council listened to Stephen, they became furious and ground their teeth at him in anger. But Stephen, full of the Holy Spirit, looked up to heaven and saw God's glory and Jesus standing at the right-hand side of God. 'Look!' he said. 'I see heaven opened and the Son of Man standing at the right-hand side of God!' With a loud cry the members of the Council covered their ears with their hands. Then they all rushed at him at once, threw him out of the city, and stoned him. The witnesses left their cloaks in the care of a young man named Saul. They kept on stoning Stephen as he called out to the Lord, 'Lord Jesus, receive my spirit!' He knelt down and cried out in a loud voice, 'Lord! Do not remember this sin against them!' He said this and died.

Acts 7:54–60 (GNB)

Reflection

Boxing Day. The day of 'recovery' after the excesses (at least in some parts of our divided world) of Christmas Day. For some a day of football matches, of horse racing, or of walking on a frosty road under a dark sky. For others a day of chasing a non-living fox through some beautiful countryside on a winter morning. For millions of us a day close to the TV, with reruns of *Dad's Army* or *The Vicar of Dibley*, or even *Strictly Come Dancing*.

The limitless wisdom of Google reminds us that the name 'Boxing Day' has numerous links to various folk traditions going back to the Middle Ages. It was a day when the occupants of the manor house gave gifts to their servants. It was also the day when the money in the church donation box was shared with the poor.

Or was it the wren, the king of birds, which indirectly gave Boxing Day its name? There is a beautiful folk memory that on the day after Christmas a wren would be captured in a box and introduced to each house in the village where he would be asked for a good year and harvest.

Many ancient legends surround this day, but in the Christian Church we have traditionally celebrated the 26th of December as St Stephen's Day. Stephen, the first martyr – stoned to death because of his commitment to the path of Christ. In T.S. Eliot's *Murder in the Cathedral* the question is raised about whether or not it is an accident that the day of the first martyr follows immediately the day of the birth of Christ: the face of suffering so intimately connected to that of rejoicing.

It's an interesting question, and not least in our own time when many of our sisters and brothers are being murdered because they are not prepared to go back on their commitment to Christ. And we can pause on this Boxing Day and remember in gratitude to God their enormous courage and faithfulness. It is a fact of our times that the number of Christian martyrs is increasing – and para-doxically, as we think of Stephen, some of them, like him, are being stoned to death even in our technological age!

The multiple traditions of Boxing Day also powerfully remind us of our ongo-ing commitments to the poor and to lasting justice in our world. In the Middle Ages a clay donation box in the village shop was shattered on Boxing Day, and the money shared out among the workers and the needy – with those who were not born with a silver spoon in their mouths like the lord of the manor. And however much the world may have changed in these last 500 years, we lose our souls if we forget this life-giving, God-inspired, Spirit-directed connection between ourselves and those in need, whether near us or far away. The more I think about it, the moment we ourselves lose this connecting thread we give up on our humanity – a humanity created in the image of God.

Boxing Day may well be a day of 'recovery' from the excesses of Christmas. A day to pause. To be gentle with ourselves. To rest our often weary souls. A day to reflect on human suffering, on human connections and on human love. To think of those who still suffer so much because they have given their lives to Jesus Christ. And to remember also our own continuing commitments to the many in our world who through no fault of their own, but rather as a result of global economic policies, find themselves in gut-wrenching poverty and need. A day to open our hearts, even if the Christmas boxes have already been opened.

Prayer

Lord of Boxing Day and of every other day,
just for a moment
may I be still
and think
of someone
somewhere in the world
who is being murdered
or tortured
because they love You
so much.

December 27th

Leith Fisher

In the beginning was the Word, and the Word was with God, and the Word was God. He was in the beginning with God. All things came into being through him, and without him not one thing came into being. What has come into being in him was life, and the life was the light of all people. The light shines in the darkness, and the darkness did not overcome it.

There was a man sent from God, whose name was John. He came as a witness to testify to the light, so that all might believe through him. He himself was not the light, but he came to testify to the light. The true light, which enlightens everyone, was coming into the world.

He was in the world, and the world came into being through him; yet the world did not know him. He came to what was his own, and his own people did not accept him. But to all who received him, who believed in his name, he gave power to become children of God, who were born, not of blood or of the will of the flesh or of the will of man, but of God.

And the Word became flesh and lived among us, and we have seen his glory, the glory as of a father's only son, full of grace and truth. (John testified to him and cried out, 'This was he of whom I said, "He who comes after me ranks ahead of me because he was before me."') From his fullness we have all received, grace upon grace. The law indeed was given through Moses; grace and truth came through Jesus Christ. No one has ever seen God. It is God the only Son, who is close to the Father's heart, who has made him known.

John 1:1–18 (NRSV)

Reflection: St John (Apostle and Evangelist)

It's past now, the great day which climaxes the welter of activities which characterises the weeks of Advent. The turkey's cooked and eaten, the presents opened, the Christmas Day verse of 'O Come, All Ye Faithful' has been sung. It's easy to miss this central truth – Christmas is about a beginning; the Incarnation means there is a new world. St John helps us remember with the words of the prologue of his gospel, the gospel passage which is the final reading of the traditional service of Nine Lessons and Carols. In the prologue he invites our hearts and minds to soar as he links the beginning which is the coming of Jesus with the beginning of creation itself. But John is always audacious, always inviting us to look higher and delve deeper. The New Testament scholar Ernst Käsemann wrote of John's gospel: 'The writer of the fourth Gospel obviously took the view that every generation has to experience the gospel afresh, and may therefore write it afresh.'[3] Given that permission, here is a brief contemporary meditation provoked by John's 'beginning'.

In the beginning

In the beginning,
the beginning, before everything,
the beginning, before anything.
In the beginning was the Word.
However it all began –
big bang or whatever ……
However it began,
there was something, some mind, someone,
something which bore the seeds
and possibilities of everything
and everyone that would ever be.

Astrophysics, genes, DNA, the lot. We say …
'In the beginning was the Word ......'
The mind of God beyond naming,
the reason of God beyond understanding,
the creative outwardness, the multiplying going-forth
of the primal mystery we dare to name 'God',
the Word of God, metaphorically spoken,
making, forming, breathing life, out of nothing ……
and things came to be.
Life was, is, will be … because
'In the beginning was the Word ......'
What was made came from God,
what was made was not God.
It was distinct, separate,
made by God, the unfathomable mind,
the mystery beyond our ken,
so alive, so mysterious as to be beyond our naming.
Yet all was made out of love … and, out of that same love
'The Word became flesh.'
In one human life,
one life like ours,
the curtain was drawn back,
through the veil we are led
to see what human powers could not reveal
that the mystery from which all came
is …
revealed as
'The Word became flesh, and we have seen his glory,
the glory as of the only begotten of the Father,

full of grace and truth.'

The Word was made flesh, shared our frailty,
shone with glory, unveiled our freedom.
In Jesus, God's word of 'Yes' to us and to all people,
God's word of 'Yes' to his world,
the 'Yes' of the new beginning in Bethlehem's stable,
the 'Yes' completed on a cross at Calvary,
the end which is another new beginning,
the death which seeds life,
the 'Yes' of his healing touch,
of his words which open eyes and minds and hearts,
of his embrace of the outsider,
of his call to follow,
of his challenge of the way things are.
The 'Yes' that pulls back the veil
and reveals a new and different face to God,
the 'Yes' that shows us that we too are made for loving and giving,
in becoming free to serve.

'We have seen his glory.'
He clarifies God,
shows us what God in us can be –
the love outpoured become the love reborn.
To see him,
to enter his way,
to know his presence,
is the beginning of wisdom ......
and life.

Prayer

Jesus, God now with us,
Jesus, Word made flesh, our flesh,
may we see your glory.
Let the fire of your life and love burn within us
and the light of your true and living way go before us
as, day by day, you bring us to a new beginning,
you who are the one who makes all things new.
Amen

December 28th

Tom Gordon

Bible reading

Thus says the Lord:
A voice is heard in Ramah,
lamentation and bitter weeping.
Rachel is weeping for her children;
she refuses to be comforted for her children,
because they are no more.
Thus says the Lord:
Keep your voice from weeping,
and your eyes from tears;
for there is a reward for your work,
says the Lord:
they shall come back from the land of the enemy;
there is hope for your future,
says the Lord:
your children shall come back to their own country.

Jeremiah 31:15–17 (NRSV)

Reflection: The age of innocents

I first came across Ally when he was 19. As the new minister in the parish, I was spending time getting the feel of the place, and found myself down at the local football pitch watching some of the boys having a kick-around. One athletic-looking lad seemed to be running awkwardly as if he was carrying an injury. Enjoying himself too much to come off, I thought. Just then, he was tackled ferociously by a flying winger. Both fell in a heap. There was much writhing about and exchanging of oaths. The big lad was first to his feet. 'Bugger me,' he shouted. 'You damn near broke ma leg. See'f it's nackered, you're fur it, nae messin'!'

With that he rolled up the bottom of his denims to examine the injured leg for damage. I expected to see severe bruising, if not an ugly, bleeding gash. What I saw, to my absolute surprise, was a flesh-coloured, shiny, artificial leg. The irate centre half rubbed the prosthesis lovingly, the way anyone would massage a damaged limb. He looked down at his still-writhing opponent, and broke into a broad grin. 'Yer aff the hook, wee man. It's no' even scratched. Jist as weel, eh?' And with his trouser leg rolled back down, he swivelled on his bad leg, called his troops back to action, and limped off into the fray once more.

The one-legged football player turned out to be Alan Morton McInnes (forever carrying the names of the legendary Glasgow Rangers' winger of the 1920s – Alan Morton, one of the 'Wembley wizards', the 'Wee Blue Devil' himself), a young leader in the local YMCA youth club. I got to know Ally very well over the years and to admire him a great deal. It turned out he'd had a leg amputated when he was five years old. He'd been messing about behind an ice-cream van and it had reversed over him. He was lucky to survive, but his leg couldn't be saved. So, from then on, he'd had a succession of artificial limbs, and, now in adult life, it didn't seem to bother him at all.

You should have seen the looks on the faces of opposition football teams when Ally and his lads from the youth club ran out for a game, with Ally's prosthesis no longer hidden behind faded denims but protruding boldly from beneath his tight, white shorts! Surprise would turn to derision. But derision always turned to respect – especially when they saw him play, and even more when they clattered into his bad leg and regularly came off worse. And Ally would often regale us with stories of the time when he worked in a local factory and would regularly purloin goodies from the production line and hide them inside his artificial leg, all to escape the scrutiny of the security guards on the way out!

But most of all, Ally was brilliant with kids. He would be seen regularly at the after-school club with a bunch of wee ones, sitting on the floor of the club room, telling them fantastic stories. One week it would be about him losing his leg in a battle with a sword-wielding giant in a far-off, exotic land. The next, it would be how he used his artificial leg to ward off a roaring lion who'd found his way into his tenement kitchen. And on another, he would be singing a made-up song:

I'm Ally, and I have to hop …
You know I can't possibly stop …
I wear this false leg …
Like a giant clothes peg …
Which I got from a novelty shop.
Boom! Boom!

The kids loved it. Singing and story-telling time with one-legged Ally was always the highlight of the week.

And it always seemed to be the most difficult kids, the most damaged ones, who related to him the most. He would spend hour after hour with kids who wore out the patience of the most tolerant of youth leaders in three-and-a-half minutes flat. But Ally had endless patience. Nothing seemed to faze him. He gave the most troublesome of youngsters all the time they needed.

In a rare quiet moment with Ally, when he took one of his occasional pauses for breath between his stories and his messing about, I asked him why it was the hardest kids, the most difficult ones that mattered most to him. He thought for a moment, and, with an unusually serious look on his face, he replied, 'It's no' me that looks for them. They aye seem tae cam' ower tae me.'

'So why you?' I asked.

There was another long pause, and an even more serious frown. 'Weel, ah lost ma innocence early on, ken? The leg, see? Ah had tae grow up affae quick, or else the ither kids would hae made mincemeat o' me. These kids have lost their innocence tae, no' wi' losin' a leg, ken, but wi' losin' ither things, like their childhood, faimlie-life, parents, freens. They've had mair chopped aff than ah ever had. They've lost mair than wan leg, they kids. Maybe they'll no' survive. But they huv tae huv a decent crack at it, eh? Maybe seein' how ah've coped can gie them anither chance.'

Alan Morton McInnes broke into a wide grin. Being serious was obviously over for now. 'Did ah ever tell ye the time ah used ma gammy leg as a plant stand fur ma granny's aspidistra?'

Innocence

In innocence I was born,
not knowing,
not wanting to know,
what this innocence meant,
and whether it was all there was.

In innocence I was broken,
not knowing,
not trying to know,
where this innocence went,
and whether it would ever return.

In innocence I was destroyed,
not knowing,
not willing to know,
when this innocence died,
and whether it had gone for good.

In innocence I was loved,
not knowing,
not able to know,
what this innocence deserved,
and whether love would make a difference.

In innocence I was held,
not knowing,
not seeking to know,
how this innocence could matter,
and whether it was worth the effort.

In innocence I was healed,
not knowing,
not asking to know,
how this innocence could be restored,
and whether wholeness was possible.

In innocence I was me,
not knowing,
not daring to know,
how this innocence had been redeemed,
and whether I was the 'me' I was meant to be.

In innocence I had hope,
not knowing,
not needing to know,
how this innocence had found comfort,
and why it kept my voice from weeping.

In innocence I had a future,
not knowing,
not searching to know,
what this innocence might face,
and when it would bring me home.

December 29th

Helen Boothroyd

Bible reading

… But whoever obeys his word, truly in this person the love of God has reached perfection. By this we may be sure that we are in him: whoever says, 'I abide in him,' ought to walk just as he walked.

1 John 2:5–6 (NRSV)

Reflection: Challenging the Powers

Today is the feast day of St Thomas Becket, the Archbishop of Canterbury murdered in Canterbury Cathedral on 29th December, 1170 by knights of King Henry II. When Becket became Archbishop eight years earlier no one would have expected him to die a martyr. He was a close ally and loyal servant of the king, holding high political office as Lord Chancellor, and had made himself unpopular in the Church by taxing it heavily on behalf of the king. But after his consecration as Archbishop, Thomas's loyalties seem to have changed. In the ongoing battle between the powers of church and state he increasingly stood against the king. We may not now have sympathy with Becket's theocratic stance, any more than we would sympathise with the autocratic stance of the king, who saw himself as absolute monarch, but we can admire the courage with which Thomas refused to recognise the state as the highest power, even when he knew that he would pay with his life. An eyewitness quoted his final words, spoken just before the fatal blow and after he had already been struck twice by knights' swords: 'For the name of Jesus and the protection of the Church, I am ready to embrace death.'

Thomas Becket's story resonates down the intervening eight centuries to find its echo in the story of another archbishop martyr whose outspoken opposition to the state he had once supported was silenced by murder in a church by agents of the regime. The repressive military dictatorship in El Salvador had welcomed the appointment of the conservative Oscar Romero as Archbishop of San

Salvador in 1977. But, like Becket, Romero's views on the political situation in his country underwent radical change. He was increasingly troubled by the murders carried out by soldiers and paramilitaries and the brutal torture inflicted by the regime's supporters on all who dared to speak out against the dictatorship, including a growing number of clerics. Romero denounced the oppression more and more strongly. In his sermon on the Sunday before he died he directed his words to each individual serving in the army: 'No soldier is obliged to obey an order that is contrary to the will of God. Nobody has to fulfil an immoral law … I beg, I ask, I order you in the name of God: stop the repression.' He had challenged the dictatorship directly by citing an authority higher than theirs. His fate was sealed. On 24th March, 1980 Romero was killed by a single bullet while celebrating Mass.

Becket and Romero had taken to heart the demanding requirement of the author of 1 John: *whoever says, 'I abide in him,' ought to walk just as he walked.* Their role model was Jesus Christ whose incarnation we celebrate in this Christmas season; the baby whose mother was told by Simeon: 'a sword will pierce your own soul too'. Words Mary must surely have remembered as thirty-three years later she stood at Jerusalem's rubbish heap watching her son being tortured to death by the Roman state because the religious and political powers felt directly threatened by his teaching and actions. Walter Wink argues compellingly that 'the Powers' executed

Jesus because his radical espousal of non-violent engagement as the God-given way to stand against evil challenged the very foundations of the 'Domination System' (based on the myth of redemptive violence) on which both their society and ours are based. [4]

Oscar Romero is not a lone martyr of modern times. I have read many times that there were more martyrs in the 20th century than in all the previous nineteen centuries since Jesus's crucifixion combined. Nor is it only Christians whose faith leads them to risk death in the cause of justice. The inspiration for almost all non-violent engagement around the world over the last 60 years came from a Hindu, Mohandas Gandhi, and a Muslim, Badshah Khan, resisting British imperialism in India.

Sadly such martyrdom continues apace in this new millennium. The courage of those people of faith who will not bow to the idol of state power, even in the face of violence, torture and death, continues to inspire and humble me. In the immediate past we have been appalled by the murders by the powers of the state of hundreds of Christians in Zimbabwe and Buddhists in Burma and Tibet who refuse to be intimidated into silence, but continue to speak out for justice for their oppressed people, right into the face of overwhelming tyranny.

I have often heard it said that non-violent resistance is utopian and cannot work in the world as it is. Yet countless examples in my own lifetime suggest otherwise. The end of apartheid, the fall of the Berlin Wall, the collapse of the Soviet Union and its empire in Eastern Europe, the fall of the Marcos dictatorship in the Philippines, the 'Orange Revolution' in Ukraine. Indeed, Wink points out that a single year, 1989-1990, witnessed successful non-violent revolutions through 'people power' in Albania, Brazil, Bulgaria, Chile, Czechoslovakia, East Germany, Hungary, Mongolia, Nepal, Poland, Romania, the Soviet Union and Yugoslavia.[5] But we should not forget that such change almost always comes at a price; a price paid by those courageous and far-sighted enough to stand publicly against evil, firm yet peaceable, many of whom have not lived to see the change that they have effected; killed by the Powers whose very existence they threatened.

I have admired from afar. Would I ever have the courage to stand firm like this myself? To refuse to bow to overwhelming earthly power even in the face of death? To live out God's new order in the here and now whatever the personal cost? I very much doubt it. Like many in the comfortable West – protected by a security blanket of overwhelming force whose ethos I may question, but the fruits of whose dominance I daily partake in – I may never be put to this test.

Relatively little is asked of me and yet even so I find it hard to have the courage to speak out for justice and to stand against discrimination, fearing unpopularity, ridicule, being different, standing out. How often have I heard the expression of prejudice against people of a particular race, religion, sexuality or nationality and failed to challenge it? How often have I spoken out for the poor, the disadvantaged and the marginalised when surrounded not by the sympathetic audience of the Iona Community, but by more hostile crowds relying on the right-wing press for their view of the world?

So I pray this Christmastide: Incarnate God, give me the courage to challenge the Powers, to speak out for justice, to stand firm against evil, in the Power of Love.

Prayer

For the way of radical non-violence incarnated in your Son Jesus.
GOD, WE THANK YOU.

For the witness and courage of the martyrs: Thomas Becket, Mohandas Gandhi, Martin Luther King, Janani Luwum, Oscar Romero, and thousands of others whose names we do not know.
GOD, WE THANK YOU.

For those today who stand firm against dictatorship, oppression and injustice in the face of imprisonment, torture and death.

GOD, WE PRAY THAT YOU WILL GRANT THEM STRENGTH AND HOPE IN THEIR RESISTANCE.

For those who use violence to hold power over others, killing and maiming those who challenge them.
GOD, WE PRAY THAT YOU WILL BRING THEM TO REPENTANCE, CHANGE AND HEALING.

For ourselves when we witness the expression of prejudice, acts of injustice or domination through violence.
GOD, GIVE US THE COURAGE TO SPEAK OUT, STAND FIRM AND DEFEND THE OPPRESSED.

In the name of Jesus: helpless baby, martyred teacher, risen saviour.
AMEN

December 30th

David Coleman and Zam Walker

Bible reading

The time came for Joseph and Mary to perform the ceremony of purification, as the Law of Moses commanded. So they took the child to Jerusalem to present him to the Lord, as it is written in the law of the Lord: 'Every firstborn male is to be dedicated to the Lord.' They also went to offer a sacrifice of a pair of doves or two young pigeons, as required by the law of the Lord.

At that time there was a man named Simeon living in Jerusalem. He was a good, God-fearing man and was waiting for Israel to be saved. The Holy Spirit was with him and had assured him that he would not die before he had seen the Lord's promised Messiah. Led by the Spirit, Simeon went into the Temple. When the parents brought the child Jesus into the Temple to do for him what the Law required, Simeon took the child in his arms and gave thanks to God:

'Now, Lord, you have kept your promise, and may you let your servant go in peace. With my own eyes I have seen your salvation, which you have prepared in the presence of all peoples: A light to reveal your will to the Gentiles and bring glory to your people Israel.'

The child's father and mother were amazed at the things Simeon said about him. Simeon blessed them and said to Mary, his mother, 'This child is chosen by God for the destruction and the salvation of many in Israel. He will be a sign from God which many people will speak against and so reveal their secret thoughts. And sorrow, like a sharp sword, will break your own heart.'

There was a very old prophet, a widow named Anna, daughter of Phanuel of the tribe of Asher. She had been married for only seven years and was now 84 years old. She never left the Temple; day and night she worshipped God, fasting and praying. That very hour she arrived and gave thanks to God and spoke about the child to all who were waiting for God to set Jerusalem free.

When Joseph and Mary had finished doing all that was required by the law of the Lord, they returned to their home town of Nazareth in Galilee. The child grew and

became strong; he was full of wisdom, and God's blessings were upon him.
Luke 2:22–40 (GNB)

Reflection: Hard print and soft memories

The New Year is sneaking up on us. And we're not ready. Not ready to let go in peace. The thirtieth day of December is neither fish nor fowl (not even cold turkey), neither here nor there. And in its unformed absence, this day may be more representative of our life than thresholds and festivals that more comfortingly focus our experience. So much of life is marking time, rather than time marked.

And now Christmas – the first one without our grandad, who died this year – has passed us by. Despite the reshuffling of the family, we've survived it, and now we are getting our breath back. For tomorrow is another day of not-quite-there.

Were folk so forced to notice, in past ages, how much we change? Living in an age that pressures us to *deny* our mortality, technology ensures we are more hopelessly immersed in the fact of mortality than ever. Confronted by our own image, in a frame or on paper, each wrinkle on your face today is in-your-face.

Do we receive the marks of our ageing as the writing of our story, our lives reflected in our features, to be worn like a medal or some other badge of honour?

Or do we regard them as the marks of shame, disclosing the reality of our changing bodies, refusing to let us pretend that nothing remains the same? In our body-obsessed, and yet body-hating, society ageing is seen as something to be avoided: the message pumped out is 'You don't have to change; you can – in fact, should – remain forever young'. All the way back to 'age shall not wither them', that poem from Remembrance Day, recalling those more decently preserved by wartime death.

Even in apparently peaceful times, the convincing lie in the back of our minds is that if you conform to the narrowly defined ideal body you might even stave off the grim reaper.

So the marks of ageing become the prison-branding of someone who has dared to live long enough to change, rather than our God-given equipment to face the unknown, and even death, with confidence.

The Old Testament is full of the fear, not of death, but of annihilation. Without descendants, Abraham believed, you vanish utterly. But trust in God schools us in letting go. In Christ the end is not the end. God finds another way.

Nonetheless … every family death shoves us sideways into a different role, and it is at times of family gatherings that we see this most acutely. All the more so now that we have set our life about with pictures. Our generation has the privilege of the merciful transition from black-and-white into colour. Old photo prints look tatty. Our childhood is chronicled by obsolete technology. It looks a long time ago, and that helps.

But still, family gatherings are compared not just by the compassionately contextualising processes of memory, but, unforgivingly, by sight. Memories are rendered sharp, unforgiving, and rock hard. The harmless-looking row of frames on the mantlepiece play a decisive part. They can hold happiness, embed guilt, yet confront us with impermanence. Remembering is one step closer to re-membering: the telescoping of past and present. Terrifying? Or the way to appreciate our place in the Story?

Did Anna, through all those years in the Temple, retain any memory of what her husband looked like? Or Simeon, perhaps, of his late wife?

Whether they did or not, in the not-quite-there time after Jesus's birth, in which the Holy Family drew breath with the aid of religious ritual, the solidarity of the elderly is an important and nourishing part of the Christmas story.

Simeon and Anna, those faithful, hopeful people, were not tormented by photos; and though their hopes seemed destined to remain unfulfilled, these are two old folk into whom we cannot read bitterness.

Part of that may be because they had help. In a way which is not described, both Anna and Simeon (tellingly not described as beggars) must have found a supportive community in which they could dream their dreams, and welcome their visions, allowing the softening of memory to heal their way through old age to the blessed release of death with fulfilment. Community enabling them to bless – with more than words – those generations whose welcome arrival takes away their fear. Generations who in their turn are ready to listen and cherish their vision.

Prayer

God, older than we can imagine, yet ever new;
God, whose Spirit is the heartbeat of a changing creation,
help us to face change.
To make transitions without fear,
having confidence that you journey with us.
Give us the courage to build community wherever we are,
valuing the vision and wisdom of whomever we encounter.
Open us to hear you speaking
through unexpected people
in unexpected places
at unexpected times,
even those we have written off.
And enable us to embrace the unknown with joy,
seeing the possibilities of your bright New World.
Amen

December 31st

John Davies

Bible reading

For everything there is a season, and a time for every matter under heaven:
a time to be born, and a time to die;
a time to plant, and a time to pluck up what is planted;
a time to kill, and a time to heal;
a time to break down, and a time to build up;
a time to weep, and a time to laugh;
a time to mourn, and a time to dance;
a time to throw away stones, and a time to gather stones together;
a time to embrace, and a time to refrain from embracing;
a time to seek, and a time to lose;
a time to keep, and a time to throw away;
a time to tear, and a time to sew;
a time to keep silence, and a time to speak;
a time to love, and a time to hate;
a time for war, and a time for peace.

What gain have the workers from their toil? I have seen the business that God has given to everyone to be busy with. He has made everything suitable for its time; more-over, he has put a sense of past and future into their minds, yet they cannot find what God has done from the beginning to the end. I know that there is nothing better for them than to be happy and enjoy themselves as long as they live; moreover, it is God's gift that all should eat and drink and take pleasure in all their toil. I know that what-ever God does endures for ever; nothing can be added to it, nor anything taken from it; God has done this, so that all should stand in awe before him.

Ecclesiastes 3:1–14 (NRSV)

Reflection: Mary Jones

Mary Jones works in a telephone call centre. It may be for a bank; it may be for directory enquiries; it doesn't really matter to us or to her – the job is the same.

From the moment she puts on her headset and poises her fingers over the computer keyboard to the moment she leaves her cubicle to head home, Mary is answering enquiries.

She is the voice at the end of the telephone queue and she is trained to deal with her customers quickly – on average, 28 seconds per call.

Mary knows that at the end of each call there's no rest – automatically the phone system notices that she is available and immediately, another caller comes on. Mary's work is a relentless series of highly structured conversations with disembodied voices in her ears; if she stops for an unscheduled break, say, two minutes for a stretch and walk around, she's at risk of losing her job, because to her employers Mary's time is money. Every last millisecond. So she mustn't waste it.

Mary is like the rest of us in our time-bound society. Mary's time is a sign of the times. We are a time-obsessed people; and rather than being liberated by it, we are possessed by time. So-called timesaving devices oppress us – think of the tension that grips people when they get into an express lift and the doors stay open a second too long; think about the causes of road rage.

And even our so-called leisure time is tainted. We get on the internet to look for the cheapest flights, months before we're due to take them. And we're always left feeling that if only we'd booked a day – or an hour – beforehand, we may have got cheaper prices. A close cousin of road rage, I've found, is 'cinema queue rage': if it looks to people like they won't get in on time, the stress levels rise and – where does the *enjoyment* go?

How we relate to time tells us so much about the sort of people we are. As we check our watches at year's end, we feel that our culture's relationship with time is an anxious, obsessive, oppressive one.

But into this culture, comes an age-old text which talks to us about time. Ecclesiastes is a good book for us to read at the turning of the year. It invites us to think again about how we see time; how we see the 'times' in which we live. It critiques them. And it suggests to us another way of living, in which time isn't a commodity which we make use of, nor a premium which we spend. Rather, time is a gift which we can receive; a gift of God which liberates and brings joy.

Ecclesiastes was written specifically for a religious people. It was written at a time of 'ease' for the people of God, a rare enough point in Israel's history where there was no conflict, where there was a measure of prosperity, where the people were just getting on with getting on with their lives.

The author called himself The Preacher; undoubtedly that was what he was; and his sermon to the people was a wake-up call for them. Because when he looked around at this religious people, this people of God, what he saw in them was complacency and cynicism.

What he said was clever because it could be taken in at least three different ways. Ecclesiastes mimics the contemporary ways of seeing time; but also offers a third way which goes beyond complacency and cynicism.

The complacent ones were happy with their lot. Probably comfortably off, their worship came easy because they could see that God was in his heaven, and all was right with their world. They saw that there was a neat order in creation – a season for everything, 'a time for every matter under heaven'.

God had made things right, God had given everyone a place in the great scheme of things and something to do, everything was 'suitable for its time' and so there was no need for any sort of moral urgency about things that seemed wrong or out of place; there was no call for them to have a lively faith because they could see nothing to challenge their easy faith.

As each year turned they saw their personal pension plans mature – the gains for their toil. The Preacher saw their complacency and called it vanity.

The cynical ones weren't so detached from the things that seemed wrong or out of place. They saw the opposition in time – that for each time of prosperity there would be a time of poverty, for each time of peace there would be war, for each time of laughter there would be a time of weeping. This they saw as proof of the death of God. They could see no connection between faith and their experience – for them, God was in his in heaven, disconnected from the world which just got on with its own life. Whatever happened, happened and God just let it happen.

So the cynics saw no need for any sort of moral urgency because they just felt that what goes around comes around, it couldn't be changed; there wouldn't be any intervention from a God who cared.

As each year turned they took things as they came, expecting little gain from their toil, doing the lottery in the vain hope of breaking the spiral, knowing full well how slender a chance they had of winning, and that even if they did they'd still be stuck in the spiral. The Preacher saw their cynicism and called it vanity.

The complacent ones took God for granted in life; the cynical ones detached God from life.

But to challenge them to see things differently, along came The Preacher preaching a message about taking life as God's gift.

The time and 'the times' are in God's hands, he said; life is a gift from God to be taken and enjoyed, he preached.

His message was neither naive nor sceptical. When he thought about the times, he saw that they were neither easy nor straightforward. That's why he portrayed life as a collection of equal opposites – good things and bad things together: birth-death; killing-healing; weeping-laughing; mourning-dancing; war-peace …

We have to attend to every matter under heaven as and when it occurs to us; for everything there is a season, and we have to adapt to each season as we adapt to the natural seasons, putting on layers in winter, putting on sun cream in summer, making sure we celebrate when times bring good news, learning the arts of comfort and tears when times are hard. God gives us the opportunity to experience all these seasons; it is God's gift that we should experience them fully and take satisfaction in the work they bring to us.

There cannot be cynicism in this perspective, because it demands a lively faith, it requires that we respond to a God who is far from detached, but fully involved in the stuff of life, giving everyone a business to be busy with.

And there cannot be complacency because part of this is a mystery to us. That's what faith is about. Trusting God without knowing why God does some things, having a sense of the order which God does bring to our times, but not knowing how and when that order will display itself.

This is how The Preacher puts it: *He has made everything suitable for its time; moreover, he has put a sense of past and future into their minds, yet they cannot find out what God has done from the beginning to the end. (Ecclesiastes 3.11)*

He goes on to affirm that *'whatever God does endures for ever; nothing can be added to it, nor anything taken from it; God has done this, so that all should stand in awe before him.'*

So we are called out of a life enclosed and stifled by time's constraints, either a life of complacency where time clocks up gains for us but God is taken for granted, or a life of cynicism where we wearily accept whatever comes because God is not involved.

We are called into a life where our time is God's time, gifted to us by God for our pleasure and fulfilment. A life which involves us in the awesome tasks of being part of God's activity in the world. A life which brings to us a sense of awe and wonder at what God is doing.

We accept this gift through prayer and a willingness to change. To be more and more open to the life and the mystery of God at all times, in each moment.

This could transform the way we are at the moment we hesitate before the lift door closes; it could alter what we let into our minds while we're queuing at the box office or the post office; it could make a great difference to our attitude when we're driving, if we begin to see all these moments as gifts to us from God.

There are many role models who help to show us how this is done, people past and present who seemed to have found the secret of living their lives to God's time.

Mary Jones is one example. Another Mary Jones, whose story comes to us from 200 years ago: another time. A young girl who lived in the shadow of Cader Idris, from the age of ten she was gripped with a desire to be able to read the Bible, filled as she was with a sense of awe and wonder at the stories that she heard from the preacher and other adults in her village.

This became her passion – but she had to wait until she was twelve before she had the chance to learn to read, and then four more years while she worked at any odd job she could find to save enough to afford to buy a bible in Welsh. At sixteen she was ready, and made the 50-mile round journey on foot to Bala to buy her Bible from the Revd Thomas Charles.

So much toil, so much time, so much waiting. A simple story, of simple faith, almost incredible to us today but nevertheless a clue about what it might mean to accept for ourselves the gift of God's time. Imagine Mary's delight as she took that Bible home. Her visit was the inspiration for Thomas Charles to establish the Bible Society, which today continues to translate the Bible into new languages for people equally as eager as Mary to read it.

No cynicism, no complacency, just a strong sense of receiving a most wonderful gift.

Prayer

God grant us such a view of our life and times as we move on into another year.

January 1st

Brian Woodcock

Bible reading

… Then I heard a loud voice call from the throne, 'Look, here God lives among human beings … There will be no more death, and no more mourning or sadness and pain. The world of the past has gone … Look, I am making the whole creation new.

Revelation 21:3–5a (NJB)

Time for a new beginning. Though my most dramatic new beginning, recently, was not 1st January but 1st September – the date of my retirement.

There would be changes anyway. But I decided to meet them head-on and do something about reducing my carbon footprint. And my pace of life. Starting with my driving.

There were those, of course, who said I should abandon the car altogether and put myself entirely at the mercy of my Senior Rail Card and bus pass. But unde-terred I learnt to ease off on the accelerator, predict next moves, become less competitive where my true character is revealed – behind the wheel. I began feel-ing safer on motorways, without the stress of overtaking, the irritation of having to slow down at roadworks, the anxiety of wondering if I had been caught on CCTV. I had gained the moral high ground.

I arrived at an Iona Community plenary, for instance, proudly announcing that I had driven at 50 all the way up the motorway and got 70 to the gallon. 'So it was you, was it?' someone retorted to much hilarity. Well, let them mock. I didn't care!

Neither did I care when they dug our road up to renew gas mains, and brought the traffic to a crawl. We live on a busy route into Bristol, which has been punctuated by temporary lights most of the year now. People take major diver-sions to avoid delays of a few minutes! But for us, the only worry was when we found ourselves in the middle of a traffic light section, and had to invent ways of backing out when we couldn't see the lights. The best way, we found, was to reverse on to the pavement, wait for the cars to stop one way, then set off before the cars started the other way. It just required a little patience. But patience was my new motto!

One morning at rush hour I reversed on to the pavement to realise the lights had moved a little, to just past our house. But the tailback stretched way down the other side of the road, and there was no way into it. So I carried on as usual: taking off when the queue at our end stopped, catching up with the last car though, then trundling along in an unhurried way till the next hold-up brought me to a halt again.

Suddenly a car was at my side, driver signalling me to wind my window down. 'Police!' he bellowed, flashing his card. 'Are you in a hurry?'

I had no idea what he meant or how to answer. But it wasn't a question. 'You overtook us at high speed, through the lights!' he shouted.

I opened my mouth like a goldfish. A car behind started hooting the unmarked car. He stuck his head out and yelled, 'Patience!' before continuing: 'That would be an £80 fine and two points on your licence.' (Or was it three?)

I realised what he thought I had done. But I wasn't in the conversation. 'Go!' he barked. 'Go! Go!'

And he sped off, leaving me bewildered and humiliated.

I wanted to explain that I had simply come out of my drive, just across the road from him. I hadn't shot round him at all. I hadn't overtaken the traffic queue on the wrong side of the road at breakneck speed. Yes, I had technically gone through lights. Just. I would have liked him to tell me how he would have backed out of my drive into a line of traffic! But any argument might have cost me £80 and two points on my licence. (Or was it three?)

I was left nursing hurt pride. And a whole lot of questions about my new life. Was my slower pace worth it if I got blamed or mocked? Were my good intentions dependent on people's appreciation? What was the point of being responsible and grey-haired if I still got taken for an immature tearaway? Especially if, under-neath, that could just possibly be true? And if it was true and I'd been found out, or it wasn't true and I'd been misunderstood, did that somehow invalidate my carbon footprint reduction?

It took a while for my pride to heal. For me to get things into proportion again, feel well-disposed towards the police, laugh at myself once more.

It took a while to realise that, come New Year, I might have to consider another life-changing resolution. It will involve a major sacrifice. But unless I am prepared to make it nothing else would really count or hold. And climate change would go its own sweet way.

Not the car. That's not what I most need to abandon. Not yet, anyway. But my pride. My ego.

Prayer

God of new beginnings,
help me make a difference in myself,
so that with your help
I may make a difference in the world.
A real difference:
in the world and in me,
at your pace,
in your peace,
God of new beginnings.

January 2nd

Thom M. Shuman

Bible reading

After eight days had passed, it was time to circumcise the child; and he was called Jesus, the name given by the angel before he was conceived in the womb.

Luke 2:21 (NRSV)

So many names ...

Author of Salvation
    eager to become
    the simple word
      rewriting all
      the trashy novels
      our lives become;

Bread of God
    leaving enough crumbs
    under the table
      for us to feed
      a world hungering
      for hope;

Firstborn of Creation
    turning the soil
    of barren chaos,
      planting the seeds
      of peace just waiting
      to be harvested by us;

Living Stone
    come to knock over
    the very foundation of death,
       watching it topple over
       into grace's embrace;

The Way
    walking up
    sin's sandy slopes,
       leaving imprints
       deep enough for
       our faltering feet;

so many …

    so we can all call you
       by name.

January 3

Norman Shanks

Bible reading

The next day John saw Jesus coming towards him and declared, 'Here is the Lamb of God who takes away the sin of the world! This is he of whom I said, "After me comes a man who ranks ahead of me because he was before me." I myself did not know him; but I came baptising with water for this reason, that he might be revealed to Israel.' And John testified, 'I saw the Spirit descending from heaven like a dove, and it remained on him. I myself did not know him, but the one who sent me to baptise with water said to me, "He on whom you see the Spirit descend and remain is the one who baptises with the Holy Spirit." And I myself have seen and have testified that this is the Son of God.'

John 1:29–34 (NRSV)

Reflection

Unlike so many of the incidents in the life of Jesus, the baptism of Jesus by John appears in all the Gospels; but the account in St John's Gospel is significantly different from the others in several respects. The Gospel opens with the familiar affirmation, wonderful and mysterious beyond comprehension, concerning the incarnate 'Word' that 'was in the beginning with God', in whom life has come into being, that is 'the light of all peoples' that the darkness did not and cannot overcome. The Gospel writer goes on to assert and explain the authority of John the Baptist, and then, here in this passage, to build on and develop the original 'Word' insight by identifying Jesus clearly and beyond doubt or challenge as the 'Son of God'. This conviction underlies the whole Gospel and both points towards and is confirmed by the resurrection and all that it signifies.

    In St John's Gospel the baptism of Jesus is described not through the eyes of the narrator as in the other Gospel accounts but by John the Baptist, thereby giving it added contemporary force, and here alone is Jesus identified not only as

God's 'Son' but also as 'the Lamb of God who takes away the sin of the world'. The image of the Lamb no doubt had connotations that were rich, varied and deep in the time and context out of which it was written and to which it was addressed – among others the Passover Lamb of the Exodus (evoking the theme of liberation), the Servant Lamb of Isaiah 53, the Lamb sacrificed in daily Temple worship, the triumphant Lamb of the book of Revelation. But I have to confess to serious doubts as to how appropriate or effective the image is (at least for those of us who live in the North and West) within the culture of today's world – predominantly urban, industrial, commercial rather than rural and agricultural. So the Communion responses, hallowed of course by long-standing tradition – 'Lamb of God, you take away the sin of the world. Have mercy upon us … Grant us your peace' (according to the version in the *Iona Abbey Worship Book*) – no longer really 'work' for me. This is partly, I readily admit, because of my theological prejudice. I do not really like the notion of sacrifice and expiation – which too easily can shade into the belief that 'God sent his Son to die on Calvary' to atone conclusively for human sin. I cannot reconcile this either with Jesus's humanity (and therefore freedom of choice) or, even more significantly, with God's love, which is limitless and unconditional and therefore demands no atoning 'price for sin'.

My problem with the lamb image, however, also has to do with the inevitable associations of vulnerability, weakness, even stupidity. This smacks too much of 'gentle Jesus, meek and mild' stuff. It is altogether too one-sided: it fails to recognise or reflect anything of the robustness, the toughness, the strength and challenging cutting-edge that is necessary to the rounded picture of Jesus we get from the Gospels. Yet of course I am aware that for our own spiritual and emotional health each one of us must learn to admit, live with, come to terms with, perhaps even to some extent overcome our weakness and vulnerability. And there is something almost counter-cultural about this: in today's society, with its dominant ethos of commodification and self-centred consumerism, there are few prizes for modesty or humility, there is a premium on status, wealth and power, on 'getting on' rather than on our relationship with others and with God. So to dwell on, even to acknowledge lamb-like vulnerability is rather like swimming against the tide.

The other day I saw a notice outside a church not far from our home, one of these 'wayside pulpit' attempts to catch the attention of passers-by. 'Why Jesus?' it said. Then 'Why not? Do you have something better?' The implication, so consistent with the spirit of our times, that Jesus is something or someone we 'have', like a possession or the latest fashionable pseudo-panacea, I find unacceptable. John the Baptist's identification of Jesus as God's 'Son', the 'Lamb of God', the incarnate 'Word' highlights and depends on a totally different dynamic: we do not possess God's truth; rather it grabs us, resist it or ignore it as we may.

Not long ago there were press reports of a letter by Albert Einstein that had just been discovered. In 1954, a year before his death, he wrote, 'The word God is for me nothing more than the expression and product of human weakness … For me the Jewish religion like all others is an incarnation of the most childish superstitions.' The article went on to suggest that, in the light of this fresh evidence, some revision appeared to be necessary of Einstein's views on religion and God – up to then regarded as agnostic but fairly positive. On the other hand, it remains clear from other statements he made that Einstein recognised the limitations of human understanding on such matters: 'The eternal mystery of the world is its incomprehensibility'; 'I believe in [the] God who reveals Himself in the orderly harmony of what exists, not in a God who concerns himself with fates and actions of human beings'; 'I want to know how God created this world. I'm not interested in this or that phenomenon, in the spectrum of this or that element. I want to know His thoughts; the rest are details.'

In other words, when Einstein talked of religion in terms of human weakness he was not dismissing its relevance, even its credibility. While as an agnostic Jew he may well have had strong reservations about the perception of Jesus as 'the Lamb of God', he spoke elsewhere of Jesus's powerful teaching and 'luminous' and 'authentic vitality'. From start to finish the striking witness and words of St John's Gospel are shot through with the dimension of mystery, no more so than in this short passage about Jesus's baptism, evoking our wonder, our worship, and our continuing striving to follow and understand.

Prayer

Living God, present in the baptism of Jesus and present still in our world, may your creative power continue to bring light to places of darkness, healing to all who suffer and transformation where there is injustice and conflict.

Jesus Christ, Lord of all that is and is to be, friend of all who are excluded, discouraged, disappointed and left behind, help us to follow in your way of compassion, generosity, justice and risk-taking.

Holy Spirit, breath of life, sustain us with your grace when times are hard, challenge us out of our preference for what is safe and comfortable, inspire us with the vision and hope of the kingdom.

January 4th

Alison Swinfen

Reflection and Bible reading

Surely a wholly unexceptional day, unless it happens to be personally exceptional? A day after the festivities of the turning of the year, a day, for many, after the return to routine. This is not the first or possibly not even the second day 'back', wherever 'back' may be, but an ordinary day in the midst of the extraordinary days of the season. We have no traditions or famous feast days on the fourth. The fourth is not the third, not a number evoking Trinity. On the fourth we are face-to-face with the ordinary, with the nothing-particularly-special-ness of life. On the fourth, we may already be regretting the breaking of resolutions made only a few days earlier, the hard task of keeping to newly chosen ways of ordering the new start. On the fourth there is no special showing, no ritual ending of the end, nothing all that new any more about a beginning, a change, just a ponderous awareness that the festivities are over, all be for the marking of their actual end.

Yet the fourth is also a border day – resolutions and festivities behind and a day of showing and knowing ahead. It's a day for finding out if all of the goodness and possibility and hope can be sustained, not just in extra-ordinary times when extra-special effort is made on an annual cycle, but in ordinary times, in the nothing-special days.

Hear now, O Israel, the decrees and laws I am about to teach you. Follow them so that you may live and may go in and take possession of the land that the Lord, the God of your fathers, is giving you. Do not add to what I command you and do not subtract from it, but keep the commands of the Lord your God that I give you.

You saw with your own eyes what the Lord did at Baal Peor. The Lord your God destroyed from among you everyone who followed the Baal of Peor, but all of you who held fast to the Lord your God are still alive today.

See, I have taught you decrees and laws as the Lord my God commanded me, so that you may follow them in the land you are entering to take possession of it. Observe them carefully, for this will show your wisdom and understanding to the nations, who will hear about all these decrees and say, 'Surely this great nation is a wise and understanding people.' What other nation is so great as to have their gods near them the way the Lord our God is near us whenever we pray to him? And what other nation is so great as to have such righteous decrees and laws as this body of laws I am setting before you today?

Only be careful, and watch yourselves closely so that you do not forget the things your eyes have seen or let them slip from your heart as long as you live. Teach them to your children and to their children after them.

Deuteronomy 4:1–9 (NIV)

Moses is looking back, remembering, pondering on the long experience of Exodus, poised, as the People of Israel are, in Moab, on the edge of the Promised Land. Up until the beginning of this chapter, the story has been one of gentle reflection, the past tense … 'we took possession', 'I assigned', 'I gave the instruc- tions', 'at that time I earnestly prayed'. We can imagine the scene, an older man, reminiscing, perhaps his mind wandering to times and places we can barely imagine. But in Chapter 4 something changes and he comes back to us – like Simeon after him – suddenly fully and prophetically present, as he was in those times he is describing. Only this time his message, and the coming reiteration of the Ten Commandments (Deut: 5), is not in Sinai, for the wilderness years, but in Moab, and for the future, for a time on the edge of the Promised Land.

Hear now, O Israel, the decrees and laws I am about to teach you. Follow them so that you may live and may go in and take possession of the land that the Lord, the God of your fathers, is giving you.

Hear now – the first imperative, followed up by more imperatives; urgent, insistent, listen to me, Israel, listen again, I'm saying it again, it's still important, it's important now. *Do not add to what I command you and do not subtract from it, but keep the commands of the Lord your God that I give you … Observe them carefully … be careful, watch yourselves closely, do not forget the things your eyes have seen or let them slip from your heart as long as you live. Teach them to your children and to their children after them.* Our God, our jealous God, demands our full attention in this text.

This is Moses speaking to God's Covenant People, the people who made the bargain with God at Sinai, the God who says, *Keep my commands and you will be my people, and I will be your God.* Here the nuance changes a little: *Follow them that you may live, that you may go into the Land, that you may take possession.* From the intangibilities of the wilderness here we stand on the verge of the tangibility of the Promised Land, and the commands are to go with us.

But only the commands – nothing more, nothing less – no adding or subtracting. And why? *For this will show your wisdom and understanding to the nations, who will hear about all these decrees and say, 'Surely this great nation is a wise and understanding people.'*

Surely this great nation is a wise and understanding people. So, God, our God, doesn't want other nations to say 'wow, aren't they amazing they have an enormous arsenal of weapons of mass destruction, hidden in the hills, half an hour up the road', or 'wow, they have such cheap flights that they have nearly destroyed the planet with their carbon emissions', or 'wow, their GDP is thousands of times that of Malawi, Sierra Leone, Burkina Faso', or even 'gosh, listen to their latest ring tones', or even 'wow, look at their national health system.' What the God of Israel *then*, and the same God – our God – today, wants others to say is *Surely this great nation is a wise and understanding people. What other nation is so great as to have their gods near them the way the Lord our God is near us whenever we pray to him?*

Wise,
understanding,
and near …
close,
as close as breathing.

This is a long way from the medieval view of an omnipotent, omniscient God somewhere in the skies, or from the god of warm, fuzzy therapeutic consumerism. Rather, as Walter Brueggemann says, 'This God is an endlessly live, demanding, giving, surprising, problematic presence in the life of Israel, one who refuses to be slotted in conveniently, but who is close, insistent, uncomfortable.'[6]

Because, of course, when we stand on the verge of something new – a new house, a new term, a new place, and new beginning, a new year – we are forever tempted to rip up the old script and start anew. And God says here, 'That's all fine but, let me just remind you of what is binding, what is covenant, what is law – what cannot ever be ripped up, if you are to be my people, and I am to be your God. And if you are to go into the world as a wise and understanding people. These are the binding laws – keep them, practise them, talk about them, think them through together. Get good at the good things.'

So this text forces us, an evangelistic people, back to the bare text and tenets of our faith. And this fourth day, this border day, the wholly unexceptional day does this for us too. The commands are terse in the Hebrew – '*lo*' meaning 'no' – no other Gods, no crooked courts, no adultery, no thieving, no murder, keep the Sabbath. It's like listening to Jesus on the subject of the Law: no adding, or subtracting, don't listen to all the pharisaical oral tradition around the text, listen to me and understand, love God, love and be just to your neighbour, as you would be to yourselves. And do it with everything you've got, because that's what it takes to bring about lives of justice and peace.

We aren't very good at keeping these commands. They are difficult to keep. This comes into sharper focus on the fourth when we perhaps realise that our grand plans and lists of resolutions are not going to be quite as easy to keep to as we'd hoped, even a few days ago. And we are particularly bad, in today's world, at remembering the Sabbath and keeping it holy. During a Christmas–Epiphany Sabbath season where we look back and often list all we've achieved, writing accounts of our last year for friends and family, making new resolutions, we are particularly bad at not-achieving, at listing all the ways in which we have just 'been', the ways we may have felt the nearness, the warm breathe of love, justice and peace. Holiday times – holy-day times – give us that Sabbath ease. Families have gathered for long, lingering meals, and walked together through the parks in cities, talking, laughing, remembering the Sabbath, and teaching this law to their children and their children's children. When I travel abroad in some countries the quietness of a lazy Sunday, and the gathering together of people for food and conversation in this way, moves me, and makes me remember; it makes me remember what my parents taught me: ... church in the morning, a special lunch, with Yorkshires, or pork scratchings – a time to play quietly, a walk to see the animals in the park, a long bath, before stories – the ones I remember were David Kossoff's *Bible Stories*, *The Lion, the Witch and the Wardrobe*, with damp hair drying by the fire, mugs of hot milk with nutmeg and mum's voice, softening us into a Sabbath sleep. If I think of what I'd like to teach children, what I try to teach those who are given into my care, it is, these days, disciplines of rest, quietness, holiday – holyday.

> and near ...
> close,
> as close as breathing.

And for us struggling to live out lives faithful and committed to justice, peace, to the integrity of creation we have a moment now to recall that God isn't inter- ested, ultimately interested in the wow-factor of our sound systems, or the numbers coming through our doors, or our doctrinal eloquence, or the colour of our carpet, God calls us to honour all our generations, to remember the Sabbath, not to idolise the risk assessments or the management structures, or the hygiene regulations as our number one Gods. No, God insists that whether we be in the wilderness, whether we be in hope and expectation of new things, or whether we be in the Promised Land itself that we observe the commands carefully. They are laws of faithful neighbourliness for days of scarcity or days of great abundance.

Compassionate not covetous, generous not acquisitive, slow to judge, quick to take time to rest, to linger, with no other gods, no investment in systems of theft or murder. Quite simply we are to live in such a way that people will know we are different, odd for God, as near to God as breathing. A wise and understanding people, living our lives for God, through commands we struggle to obey and to make again anew in the ordinariness of our everyday lives.

Perhaps,
after
the holiness
is done,
you are not
particularly
extraordinary
after all.

You come
as familiar
as the
sound of
the latch
lifting
telling me
the journey is over
and this is
home.

As ordinary
as day shading
into evening.

Regular as
clockwork.

As unassuming
as the
rise and fall
of breathing,

not so much
new as
tenderly normal

the delight of
small things

words waiting
in my mother's
tongue

a table

bread

the
curve of
a cup
braced
in my
working hands.

January 5th

Ian M. Fraser

Bible readings

In the time of King Herod, after Jesus was born in Bethlehem of Judea, wise men from the East came to Jerusalem, asking, 'Where is the child who has been born king of the Jews? For we observed his star at its rising, and have come to pay him homage.' When King Herod heard this, he was frightened, and all Jerusalem with him; and calling together all the chief priests and scribes of the people, he enquired of them where the Messiah was to be born. They told him, 'In Bethlehem of Judea; for so it has been written by the prophet: "And you, Bethlehem, in the land of Judah, are by no means least among the rulers of Judah; for from you shall come a ruler who is to shepherd my people Israel."'

Then Herod secretly called for the wise men and learned from them the exact time when the star had appeared. Then he sent them to Bethlehem, saying, 'Go and search diligently for the child; and when you have found him, bring me word so that I may also go and pay him homage.' When they had heard the king, they set out; and there, ahead of them, went the star that they had seen at its rising, until it stopped over the place where the child was. When they saw that the star had stopped, they were overwhelmed with joy. On entering the house, they saw the child with Mary his mother; and they knelt down and paid him homage. Then, opening their treasure chests, they offered him gifts of gold, frankincense and myrrh. And having been warned in a dream not to return to Herod, they left for their own country by another road.

Matthew 2:1–12 (NRSV)

Reflection

The Christmas card industry does its best to perpetuate a misinterpretation of scripture. There were no kings presenting gifts to the infant Jesus. There were magi or astrologers or wise men making an offering of their tools of trade, discarding them before a greater power whom they now worshipped as the true bearer of light and truth. They went back a different way to a different life.

How did kings nose their way in, as did the proverbial camel into the proverbial tent? The story was conflated with Old Testament references. The most potent of these is in Isaiah 60 – the promise given to Jerusalem:

> *Arise, shine, Jerusalem, for your light has come;*
> *and over you the glory of the Lord has dawned.*
> *Though darkness covers the earth and dark night the nations,*
> *on you the Lord shines and over you his glory will appear;*
> *nations will journey towards your light*
> *and kings to your radiance …*
>
> *Camels in droves will cover the land,*
> *young camels from Midian and Ephah*
> *all coming from Sheba laden with gold and frankincense,*
> *heralds of the Lord's praise. (Is 60:1–3;6)*

This comes against a background where evil had seemed to triumph:

> *There was no justice, and when the Lord saw it he was displeased.*
> *He saw that there was no help forthcoming*
> *and was outraged that no one intervened;*
> *so his own arm worked salvation for him*
> *and his own righteousness sustained him. (Is 59:15,16)*

These prophecies of 'Third Isaiah' refer to events located somewhere between 516 and 444 BC. Kings will journey, attracted by the glory of Jerusalem, when exiles return from Babylonian banishment to restore it from its ruined state. Gold and frankincense are mentioned among many, many treasures which will be brought to enhance its life.

Kings and offerings far back in history have been inserted in the birth of Jesus narratives, where they are out of context!

A very ancient tradition did not interpret the offerings as gifts in our Christmas-giving sense. They were offerings all right, but of the kind that the IRA made when they handed over weapons to be decommissioned. Frankincense suggested the mystique which gave a priestly caste, 'those in the know', power. Myrrh suggested what Robert Burns called 'the hangman's whip tae haud the wretch in order': the deference proper to those who are believed to have control of one's fate in the afterlife. Gold: the false god and a reward for services rendered. These sorcery tools of trade were discarded at Jesus's feet, abandoned by wise men who recognised that they were encountering a new reality which, from that time on, would direct their ways. They returned by a different route, both to avoid Herod and to follow this new way.

In a poem, I put it thus:

Magi versed in occult arts
note strange portents in the sky.
The Fiend to appease?
Evil transcendent?
– the omen sublime
a Child Ascendant!
    Camels saddled, tools of trade
    packed, they trace a path star-made,
    eyes fixed high, discarding their charts.

Questions shake Jerusalem
(voiceless myrrh, frankincense, gold)
'Where's the Great Lord
whose heralded birth
displaces the stars
unhinges the earth?'
Priests and scribes consult, agree:
    Herod says, 'I'll bend the knee –
    southward hold, to Bethlehem.'

Rapt, they face the world's one Light.
Changed, they cast before the Son,
gold, the seducer,
death-witching myrrh,
priestly mystique limned
in smoke from the fir
broken is the Devil's sway:
    warned, they choose a different way.
    Life is begun! The blind have sight!

Prayer

Lord God,
we give thanks for those who live by the light they see,
and look for more light, ready to journey into truth.
Enable us to share with them the light we have
and also to stand teachable before their experience.

Free us to make our coming into the presence of a child a converting event.

Save us from making tradition serve our longing for security
when you, Lord God,
are making all things new, bringing tradition alive.

We ask it in Jesus Christ's name. Amen

January 6th

An all-age celebration for Epiphany

Ruth Burgess

Many churches hold a party on the Feast of Epiphany. The following liturgy can stand on its own with a conventional sermon/reflection, or it could split after the readings, with activities taking the place of a reflection. A list of possible half-hour activities is given at the end of the liturgy. These can be expanded or added to as your resources allow. Activities should be open to all ages. Elements of the liturgy could be used at the beginning or end of a party.

You will need as many stars as there are participants in the liturgy. They need to be hung on a Christmas tree or on cut branches in an accessible place in the worship area.

The main theme of the liturgy is that of wonder and of 'following your star' – of 'going for it', of travelling with God the adventure of life.

The liturgy should be led by a number of voices.

Opening responses

In the beginning was darkness
AND GOD MADE THE EARTH AND THE HEAVENS
AND SET THE STARS IN THE SKY

In the beginning was chaos
AND GOD CREATED ORDER AND BEAUTY
AND GAVE EACH STAR ITS NAME

In the beginning was discord
AND ALL THE STARS SANG TOGETHER
AND THE ANGELS SHOUTED FOR JOY

Song: Christ, Mighty Saviour (CH4 216) or All Creatures of Our God and King (CH4 147)

God our Maker,
you fill us with wonder,
you welcome us with love.

Jesus our friend,
you call us to walk with you,
you teach us justice and truth.

Holy Spirit our wisdom,
you are in us and around us,
you question us and keep us right.

Holy God,
in your presence we are amazed.
You made everything that is:
deep seas, high mountains,
stars we are unable to count.
You made everything
and you know our names.
You are interested in who we are
and what we do and who we love.

We are quiet before you now,
words and faces and wonder filling our minds,
memories dancing in and out of our being.

We thank you for your gifts,
for your love.

We are happy for the people we have helped.
We are sad for the times we have hurt others
and hurt ourselves.
We are sorry for the messes we have made.

Listen to the words of Jesus:
'I am the bright morning star
I am the light of the world
I love you
I forgive you
Come and walk with me.'

Thanks be to God. Amen

Readings: Sirach/Ecclesiasticus 43:1–10, Psalm 148 (sung version: Glory to God above CH4 105), Matthew 2:1–12

Song (can be omitted if a sung version of the psalm is used)

Activities (see list)

Or a reflection on the readings and on 'following your star' …

Song (or, if you have been having activities, share briefly what you have done: songs … stars you've seen … a banner … some drama or reflection … poems … food …)

Creed

WE BELIEVE IN GOD THE MAKER,
WHO CREATED HEAVEN AND EARTH,

STAR-MAKER, SINGER, SOURCE OF LIFE.

WE BELIEVE IN JESUS THE STORYTELLER,
WHO WALKED THE ROADS OF GALILEE,
BEFRIENDER, QUESTIONER, SOURCE OF TRUTH.

WE BELIEVE IN THE HOLY SPIRIT,
WHO IS AS CLOSE TO US AS OUR HEARTBEAT,
CHALLENGER, COMFORTER, SOURCE OF JOY.

WE BELIEVE THAT GOD IS IN OUR MIDST,
CALLING US TO CARE FOR ONE ANOTHER
AND TO WORK FOR JUSTICE AND PEACE.

WE LOOK FOR THE LIGHT OF GOD
TO SHINE ON US AND IN US
THROUGH ALL THE ADVENTURES
OF OUR NIGHTS AND DAYS. AMEN

Song: Christ Be Our Light (CH4 543)

Intercessions

God of earth and heaven,
you love your creation,
you love us;
hear us now
as we bring you our concerns and our prayers:

We pray for the earth, that we may live on it responsibly.
Teach us to recognise and respect you in the wonders you have made.

God, in your mercy,
HEAR OUR PRAYER

We pray for those who help us to wonder – for scientists, astronomers, designers
of telescopes and planetariums, artists, poets and storytellers.
God, in your mercy,
HEAR OUR PRAYER

We pray for those who will sleep under the stars tonight – for travellers, refugees,
explorers, for those fleeing danger.
God, in your mercy,
HEAR OUR PRAYER

We pray for those who are ill or in trouble or in any kind of need …
We pray for/remember those who have died,
and for those who love them and miss them …
God, in your mercy,
HEAR OUR PRAYER

We pray for ourselves, that you will give us dreams
and the courage to follow them …
God, in your mercy,
HEAR OUR PRAYER

God of beauty and mystery,
you love each one of us
and we are wonderfully and intricately made.
Be close to us in our tears and our laughter.
Keep us loving and just and full of wonder.
Fill us with life.
AMEN

Action: Collecting a star from the tree

Accompany the action with music from music group, variations on Twinkle, Twinkle, Little Star, etc.

Blessing (while holding stars)

May God, the three in one, bless these stars.
May they remind us of our call to wonder and to adventure.
AMEN

May God, the Maker, bless us
and fill us with hope and with courage.
AMEN

May God in Jesus, the bright morning star, bless us
and shine in our lives.
AMEN

May God, the Holy Spirit, dance among us
and hallow us with wisdom and with joy.
AMEN

Song: As with Gladness Men of Old (CH4 326)

Possible activities

Stargazing – outdoors, using a telescope, binoculars, looking through cardboard tubes/toilet roll holders. Have a quiz about stars and planets. Look at a star map for winter.

Making banners – 'I am the bright morning star', 'Twinkle, twinkle', 'God hung the stars in the sky', 'Every star shall sing a carol' …

Decorating stars – Use a 5-pointed star template to make stars. Attach a looped hanger to the Christmas tree to hang the stars on. Decorate the stars with felt pens, glue and glitter, quick-drying paint, finger paint, spray paint, gummed stars, shapes …

Music/singing – Play some music from *The Planets Suite* by Gustav Holst. Sing some songs about stars. Use percussion to create music … Practise a version of Twinkle, Twinkle, Little Star to play later in the liturgy; Mozart has variations based on Twinkle, Twinkle. (The text of Twinkle, Twinkle is by Jane Taylor and contains five verses.)

Thinking/dreaming – Look at Sydney Carter's song 'Every Star Shall Sing a Carol'. Which images in the carol do you find attractive? Is there anything in the carol that makes you feel uncomfortable? What kind of questions does the carol make you ask?

Look at some Bible verses about stars – Job 9:7; Job 38:7; Psalm 147:4; Sirach/Ecclesiasticus 43:1–10; 1 Corinthians 15:41; Revelation 22:16

Poetry/drama – Dramatise a version of Matthew 2:1–12; read 'The Coming of the Magi' by T.S. Eliot; read something from *The Little Prince* by Antoine de Saint Exupéry, or from other star poems/stories. Write a star poem.

Food and drink – Ice/decorate moon- and star-shaped cakes and biscuits. Make star-shaped open sandwiches. Make fruit juice; cut fruit into cross-sections and look for star shapes.

Songs from CH4 (*Church Hymnary 4*, John L. Bell (ed.), Canterbury Press):
144   I Love the Sun
147   All Creatures of Our God and King
148   The Spacious Firmament on High
151   All You Works of God
216   Christ, Mighty Saviour, Light of All Creation
288   Creator of the Stars of Night
323   The First Nowell
326   As with Gladness Men of Old
463   Fairest Lord Jesus
540   I Heard the Voice of Jesus Say
543   Christ Be Our Light

Songs from elsewhere:
Can You Count the Stars that Brightly Twinkle in the Midnight Sky
Every Star Shall Sing a Carol
If I Was a Beautiful Twinkling Star
Twinkle, Twinkle, Little Star
We Three Kings of Orient Are
When a Knight Won His Spurs

Epiphany

Jan Sutch Pickard

Bible reading

*Then they returned to their own country by another route, for they had been warned
in a dream not to go back to Herod. Matthew 2:1–12 (REB)*

Reflection: Dreams and angels

At the turn of the stairs in the Abbey in Iona, there used to be a beautiful and
intriguing pewter plaque. Although the casting was modern, the style and the
story were much older, for it was based on a Romanesque carving in Autun,
Burgundy, made in the 12th century by a craftsman called Gislebertus.

Imagine the picture, which guests in the Abbey and Community members
would have seen each night as they went to their beds: Here are the three Magi –
astrologers, wise men – asleep in one bed. Maybe they are kings, too, for their
heads on the pillow are crowned. Shakespeare wrote 'Uneasy lies the head that
wears a crown' – and they can't be very comfortable. But this is not meant to be
photographic realism, but to convey to us the depth and drama of the scene.
Next to the bed stands an angel, with spreading wings and a halo so big that it
breaks out of the frame of the picture. The angel's magnificent gown spreads out
to form a bedcovering for the Magi, so it is part of their sleep and their dream. But
the angel is wide awake, pointing urgently with his left index finger to the star
which has led them to this place, to the Christ-child. His right index finger touches
the hand of one of the sleeping Magi. And, as though an electrical impulse had
run up the bare arm lying on the coverlet, the eyes of the sleeping man are opening – taking in the dream's message:

'*… they had been warned in a dream not to go back to Herod.*'

Imagine what will happen when they wake up. This is a story of learned men,
who know about the past and the future, who have focused together, maybe for
years, on a research project, who have made an arduous journey across frontiers,

who have found what they were searching for, a newborn king, and who have knelt (grown men before a child) to pay homage, as they delivered generous and symbolic gifts. On their journey they have been given one more task – to go back and tell Herod, the real power in that land, all that they have seen.

It would be logical, in alien territory, to retrace their steps. But now they have been warned to go back another way. As astrologers they know the importance of symbols, the meaning of dreams. Would important, busy men today be as willing to contemplate a change of plan, to abandon the logic of power politics and self-preservation? Are these Magi wise enough to be foolish? Having followed a star, will they follow the leading of a dream?

Epiphany means a manifestation – a discovery, a showing, bringing into the light of day, seeing plainly. In the helpless child in his mother's arms, they saw the Messiah: a powerful moment of epiphany. And now this dream shows them something else. It is a little epiphany, a way of seeing that everything is not as it seems: that there is another level of truth, and a different way home.

At what points in your life have you seen things in a new light, been turned round, discovered the importance of taking a different way?

Going home another way

At the turn of the stairs
between waking and sleeping
and waking again
between action and reflection
God speaks to us
in riddles and symbols
and half-remembered stories:
where angels have their feet on the ground
and wise men are foolish.

Even in mystery
there is epiphany
God speaks to us –
reminds us of the stars
gives us glimpses of the way ahead.

At the turning of the year
is a time to look forward,
while holding on
to those moments in the year past
when we suddenly became aware
of God with us.
We waste time if we look back in anger or regret,
or forward in fear.
Though these days are short,
they can dazzle with their brightness.
Epiphany, a season of clear-seeing:
life in perspective, with all its possibilities,
before the diary fills up –
an unwritten page; a door opening;
a field of snow untrodden.

God of dreams and discoveries,
at this turning point in our lives
may your epiphany open our eyes:
may we be wise enough
to become fools for Christ's sake,
and as we step into another year
of our journey home to you,
may we find courage to go a different way. Amen

The Night Stair

Quiet as thick
flakes of snow. Quiet
as the rising and falling
of a child's sleep. Quiet
as the abbey church at
candlefall when
Amens are said,
and on the air,
before the latch drops,
behind the night stair,
the last echo of God
breathing in our
prayer.

Alison Swinfen

Christmastide themes

Bible readings, quotes, prayers and actions

Neil Paynter

LIGHT

Psalm 27:1
Matthew 28:3

Light a candle, don't just curse the darkness.

A Chinese saying

Prayer

Jesus Christ, light of the world,
help me to work to bring hope, healing and justice
to those who are suffering,
in my neighbourhood and
in the neighbourhood of the world.
Amen

Action:

There used to be a tradition during the Christmas season/wintertime of burning a yule log/candle. This, folk believed, helped to bring light back into the dark world.

Light a candle of hope for a place of oppression and darkness in our world today. In 2009, think about the situation in Tibet, Burma, Zimbabwe …

DARKNESS

Psalm 139:11–12
2 Corinthians 4:6

'Because even in the darkest times, I found, there is a seed of light.'

A person with mental health challenges

Prayer

God, help me to find the seed of light
buried
in even the darkest times.
Amen

Action:

Stand out in a country field and gaze up at the stars …

THE BOXING DAY TSUNAMI, 2004

1 Corinthians 12:26
Micah 6:8

The utterly random nature of so much of life is about the only certainty we have between birth and death. It is a futile debate to ask why life is random, for we can only be sure that it is. It is futile to speculate about what life would be were there no such things as earthquakes, tidal waves, droughts and other vagaries of the awesome power of nature. It's like trying to wonder what life would be like if there was a certain lifespan, say we all lived to 70 where none died young, or lived to be 100. All we can say is that it would not be life as we know it. Life as we know it has a random power beyond our controlling. There is also a different random-ness of our human making which we call sin and which cumulatively, through the greed and wickedness of some, condemns others to a lifetime of unwarranted and unavoidable poverty and fragility ...

Erik Cramb, from a letter

Prayer

God,
help me to remember
and to act upon the fact that
people in the world go on suffering
long after they have disappeared
from my TV screen.
Amen

Action:

Save the Children
www.savethechildren.org

Oxfam
www.oxfam.org.uk

GIFTS

Acts 20:35
1 Corinthians:12:31

I offered up a special prayer, a prayer which came with tears and anguish, that some way would open up for me to use what talents I possessed for my fellow workers, for the poor.

Dorothy Day, The Long Loneliness

Prayer

Each thing we have received,
from you it came, O God.
Each thing for which we hope,
from your love it will be given.
Kindle in our hearts within
a flame of love to our neighbours,
to our foes, to our friends, to our loved ones all.
Amen

Gaelic traditional

THINGS

John 10:10
1 Timothy 6:7

Create a society where people matter more than things.

Archbishop Desmond Tutu

Prayer

Christ, help me to live more simply
and with greater faith in you. Amen

LONELINESS

Isaiah 43:1–4
John 14:18

Language … has created the word 'loneliness' to express the pain of being alone.
And it has created the word 'solitude' to express the glory of being alone.

Paul Tillich

Prayer

O God, early in the morning I cry to you.
Help me to pray
and to concentrate my thoughts on you:
I cannot do this alone.
In me there is darkness,

but with you there is light;
I am lonely, but you do not leave me;
I am feeble in heart, but with you there is help;
I am restless, but with you there is peace.
In me there is bitterness, but with you there is patience;
I do not understand your ways,
but you know the way for me …
Lord, whatever this day may bring,
your name be praised.

Dietrich Bonhoeffer, a prayer written in Tegel prison

Action:

Think of people around the world who are in prison … who are on death row … who are under house arrest for their political views … Aung San Suu Kyi, Burma's democracy leader, has been under house arrest in Burma for over 12 years.

The Burma Campaign
www.burmacampaign.org.uk

Amnesty International
www.amnesty.org

PEACE ON EARTH

Isaiah 2:1–4
Matthew 5:9

The 10 countries with the highest military expenditure in 2007 (US$ billion):

1. USA, 547
2. UK, 59.7
3. China, 58.3 (estimated figure)
4. France, 53.6
5. Japan, 43.6
6. Germany, 36.9
7. Russia, 35.4 (estimated figure)
8. Saudi Arabia, 33.8
9. Italy, 33.1
10. India, 24.2

Figures from the Stockholm International Peace Research Institute (SIPRI), www.sipri.org

Think about how all that money (maybe some of it your taxes) could have been used: food, hospitals, doctors, nurses, antiretroviral AIDS drugs, finding a vaccine for malaria, alleviating poverty, housing, schools, youth centres, sustainable energy, pensions, the arts, beauty …

Does it make you feel sad? Does it make you feel angry?

Think about all that money being spent year after year, year after year … on death.

What a colossal, immoral, insane waste.

Martin Luther King wrote: 'A nation that continues year after year to spend more money on military defence than on programs of social uplift is approaching spiritual doom.'

Prayer

O God,
lead us from death to life, from falsehood to truth.
Lead us from despair to hope, from fear to trust.
Lead us from hate to love, from war to peace.
Let peace fill our hearts, our world, our universe.

The universal prayer for peace

Action:

Campaign Against the Arms Trade
www.caat.org.uk

Campaign for Nuclear Disarmament
www.cnduk.org

RESOLUTIONS/MAKING DECISIONS

Exodus 14:15
Philippians 4.6–7

'You don't get to choose how you're going to die. Or when. You can only decide how you are going to live. Now.'

Joan Baez

Prayer

God, grant me the serenity to accept the things I cannot change,
courage to change the things I can,
and the wisdom to know the difference.

Prayer from Alcoholics Anonymous

HOSPITALITY

1 Kings 17:7–16
Hebrews 13:1–2

'I feel like a second-class citizen.'

A Muslim in Britain, 2005

Prayer

Pray for all who are not welcomed:
refugees and asylum seekers;

all who are homeless …

Jesus, you were a refugee.
You knew what it was like
to wander the streets and countryside
without any shelter.

Help me to recognise you in the stranger
and in the people I see every day.
Amen

Action:

Refugee Action
www.refugee-action.org.uk

The Simon Community
www.simoncommunity.org.uk

WASSAILING

Genesis 1:11–13
John 15:5

There were many different wassailing traditions. In areas of England where cider was made, folk would drink and sing to the health of apple trees in hopes of producing a good harvest and to chase away evil spirits:

Wassaile the trees, that they may beare
you many a plum and many a peare:

For more or lesse fruits they will bring,
as you do give them wassailing …

Robert Herrick (1591-1674), from **Ceremonies of Christmas Eve**

Prayer

Meditate on this Cree Indian saying:

Only when the last tree has died
and the last fish has been caught
and the last river has been poisoned
will we realise
that we can't eat money

Action:

Go out with a group and wassail a tree. Give thanks for God's amazing creation; sing a song to chase away the evil spirits of human greed, disconnection and apathy. Plant a tree (if you live somewhere where this can be done in winter-time). Or plant a seed, and in the spring replant it outside. Make a prayer tree or a peace tree.

Learn names of trees: become rooted in the place you live. Look at the shapes of different leaves. Look at the veins in different leaves and then at the veins in your hands. Hug a tree – the women of the Chipko movement in India hug trees to keep them from being cut down. Hugging a tree is a matter of life and death for them.

The Soil Association
www.soilassociation.org

The Greenbelt Movement
www.greenbeltmovement.org

NEW WAYS TO TOUCH THE HEARTS OF ALL

Isaiah 43:18–21
John 13:34–35

Christ is always at least one step ahead of us.

A saying

O God, who gave to your servant Columba the gifts of courage, faith and cheer-fulness, and sent people forth from Iona to carry the word of your gospel to every creature: grant, we pray, a like spirit to your church, even at this present time. Further in all things the purpose of our community, that hidden things may be revealed to us, and new ways found to touch the hearts of all. May we preserve with each other sincere charity and peace, and, if it be your will, grant that this place of your abiding be continued still to be a sanctuary and a light. Through Jesus Christ. Amen

Prayer of the Iona Community, Iona Abbey Worship Book

Action:

Look at the work of these prophetic organisations:

ATD Fourth World
www.atd-uk.org

GalGael Trust
www.galgael.org

Braendam Link
www.braendam.org.uk

Resurgence magazine
www.resurgence.org

Probably you know of other organisations and people, Christian and otherwise, working in prophetic ways. How might you get more involved in God's work?

THE NEW MILLENNIUM

At the beginning of the year 2000, there was a palpable feeling of hope among activists that the world's heavily indebted countries would finally have their debts cancelled.

After almost ten years now, $88 billion of poor country debt has been cancelled. However, according to the Jubilee Debt Campaign, at least $400 billion of debt still needs to be cancelled 'if the world's poorest countries are to combat the challenge of global poverty'.

Leviticus 25:10–14
Luke 4:16–21

You think you're too small to make a difference? Then you've obviously never slept in the same room as a mosquito.

African proverb

Prayer

Our Father in heaven,
hallowed be your name,
your kingdom come,
your will be done on earth as in heaven,
give us today our daily bread,
forgive us our sins
as we forgive those who sin against us,
save us in the time of trial
and deliver us from evil,
for the kingdom, the power
and the glory are yours,
now and for ever. Amen.

Action:

Write your MP/government representative, urging them to take action on the debt crisis.

The Jubilee Debt Campaign
www.jubileedebtcampaign.org.uk

THE LORD OF MISRULE

Acts 17:6
1 Corinthians 1:25

'God give them wisdom that have it; and those that are fools, let them use their talents.'

Feste, **Twelfth Night,** *Shakespeare*

Prayer

Christ has come to turn the world upside down:
TO HUMBLE THE POWERFUL AND TO LIFT UP THE LOWLY.
Christ has come to turn the tables:
TO TOPPLE VAIN IDOLS AND TO STAND WITH THE POOR.
Christ has come to proclaim God's kingdom:
TO FEED THE HUNGRY,
TO LIBERATE THE OPPRESSED,
TO STRENGTHEN THE WEARY,
TO SET THE PRISONERS FREE.
Christ has come to turn the world upside down:
TO OVERTHROW THE PRESENT ORDER
WITH A REVOLUTION OF LOVE.

Responses from **The Iona Abbey Worship Book**

Action:

Look at the work of these organisations and individuals; folk who use humour to help bring healing and justice to the world – to shake things up, to turn the world upside down.

Gesundheit Institute
www.patchadams.org

Amnesty International
www.amnesty.org (search for 'Stand Up For Freedom')

Comedy Relief
www.comicrelief.com

Mark Thomas
www.markthomasinfo.com

Michael Moore
www.michaelmoore.com

St Francis called himself 'God's jester'. How might you be more of a 'holy fool'?

HANGOVERS

John 2:1–10
Acts 2:1–13

You'll never enjoy the world aright
'til the sea itself floweth
in your veins and you are clothed
with the heavens
and crowned with the stars

Thomas Traherne, English mystic (1636-1674)

Prayer

O God, make me drunk with wonder,
high on mystery …
Make me your drunk mystic, O God,
weaving and dancing around everywhere
singing about your Love,
your sweet Love,
your sweet, intoxicating Love …

SACRED AND SECULAR

Exodus 3:5
John 1:14

Spirituality is the place where prayer and politics meet.

Kate McIlhagga

Prayer

In you all things consist and hang together:
The very atom is light energy,
the grass is vibrant,
the rocks pulsate.
All is in flux; turn but a stone and an angel moves.

George MacLeod, from **The Whole Earth Shall Cry Glory: Iona Prayers**

PAST, FUTURE, LIVING IN THE NOW

2 Corinthians 5:17
Hebrews 12:1–2
Matthew 6:25–34

Every person is Christ to me, and since there is only one Jesus, that person is the one person in the world at that moment.

Mother Teresa

Prayer

Neither eight hundred years ago, nor yesterday
are these our flesh and bones redeemed;
but now in this moment
as we put our trust in Thee
we are made new.
New creatures we become
The inner flesh of our immortal bodies – vibrant to eternity.

George MacLeod

REST

1 Kings 19:14
Matthew 11:28

Look within.
Be still.
Free from fear and attachment.
Know the sweet joy of the way.

The Buddha, from The Dhammapada

Prayer

God, give me a moment to be still:
to listen for your voice in my heart.

Peter Millar

THE SEASONS

Genesis 1:14
Psalm 74:17

Live each season as it passes; breathe the air, drink the drink, taste the fruit, and resign yourself to the influences of each ... For all nature is doing her best each moment to make us well. She exists for no other need. Do not resist her ...

Henry David Thoreau, Walden

Prayer

I love rhythm
spring, summer, autumn, winter
Lent, Easter, Advent, Christmas,
Jack Frost, bluebells, full moon, conkers …

Thanks for all the seasons, God.

Ruth Burgess

Action:

Stop Climate Chaos
www.stopclimatechaos.org

Friends of the earth
www.foe.co.u

SNOW

Psalm 51:7
Matthew 28:3

'God's an artist who loves infinite detail – just look at a snowflake!'

Source unknown

Prayer

God, thank you for the snowflakes that fall
and land

on my face
on my nose
on my eyelashes …

I hold out my tongue and receive … communion.

Make me a clean heart, O God.
Set a new and right spirit within me

Make me a joyful child.
Make me a joyful child.

Action:

Make paper snowflakes. Be a child again. Do this activity with children. If there's snow where you live, go out and make a snow angel, a snowman, a snow fort … If people think you're crazy – so what! If people can't play – they're the crazy ones. Shovel an old woman's/man's walkway for free. Take a walk in the snow. Do something that makes you feel free and alive, and thank God for feeling, being alive; do something that connects you to the earth and sky.

Think of folk in countries where it's summertime now. Pray for folk in Africa, Asia … Pray that they might have lasting peace; and where there isn't peace, pray for a thawing of hostilities and an end to conflict and fighting.

GOING BACK TO WORK/SCHOOL

Proverbs 2:1–5
Ecclesiasticus 38

'Only a demanding common task builds community.'

George MacLeod, Founder of the Iona Community

Prayer

O Christ, the Master Carpenter,
who at the last, through wood and nails,
purchased our whole salvation,
wield well your tools in the workshop of your world,
so that we who come rough-hewn to your bench
may here be fashioned to a truer beauty of your hand.
We ask it for your own name's sake.
Amen

A prayer from the Iona Community, **Iona Abbey Worship Book**

Action:

Church Action on Poverty
www.church-poverty.org.uk

The Socialist Party
www.socialistparty.org.uk

WRITING THANK YOU CARDS/LETTERS

Proverbs 17:17
1 Thessalonians 5:18

If the only prayer you ever say in your entire life is thank you, it will be enough.

Meister Eckhart

Prayer

Dear God,
Thank you for family and friends.
Love,

Action:

Write your thank you cards/letters.

SOME CHRISTMASTIDE SAINTS

St Basil the Great (4th century, Asia Minor, January 2)

As well as being a leading theologian and orator in his time, St Basil led a life of action – he helped in soup kitchens, worked in famine relief, cared for children …

Luke 2:1–7
Psalm 113:2–8

The bread which you do not use is the bread of the hungry; the garment hanging in your wardrobe is the garment of him who is naked; the shoes that you do not wear are the shoes of the one who is barefoot; the money that you keep locked away is the money of the poor; the acts of charity that you do not perform are so many injustices that you commit.

St Basil

Prayer

Jesus, help me to put my ideas
into action
and not just talk about it.
Amen

Elisabeth Ann Seton (19th century, America, January 4)

Elisabeth Ann Seton founded the Sisters of Charity, the first American religious community for women, and established the first American Catholic orphanage. She did all this work while at the same time keeping a house and raising five children.

John 14:13–14
Romans 12:1–2

The first end I propose in our daily work is to do the will of God; secondly, to do it in the manner he wills it; and thirdly, to do it because it is his will.

Elisabeth Ann Seton

Prayer

Most high, glorious God,
enlighten the darkness of my heart,
and give me right faith,
certain hope,
and perfect charity,
wisdom and understanding,
Lord, that I may carry out
your holy and true command.
Amen

St Francis

St Simon Stylites (5th century/Syria/January 5th)

St Simon Stylites is 'famous' for having lived on a platform on top of a pillar for thirty-seven years – a major feat of asceticism. Although Simon lived 'above the world', he was apparently still very much engaged in it. People with problems visited him regularly, and he was always available to them.

Matthew 14:13–14
Luke 4:1–13

This emphasis on withdrawal formed a strong part of the Celtic tradition. Columba would retreat to Hinba (an island still not clearly identified) as Jesus would retire to a mountain or desert. But prayer and reflection were balanced by involvement in the world's affairs. Columba, whose lineage might have allowed him to become High King of Ireland, acted as powerbroker between warring dynasties and tribes. Holiness for him was not in being separated from the world but in being separated for God in the world, a commitment which called both for involvement and reflection, as it does today.

Ian M Fraser, from **Celebrating Saints**

Prayer

May prayer feed my actions,
and may my actions
help to feed the world.

St Apollinaria/Dorotheus (Early Christian, January 5, 6)

Apollinaria was a woman who, in order to become part of the organised 'Church' of her day, changed her name and lived her life as a man.

John 20:18
1 Samuel 18:1–5

'If you can't be yourself in church, in front of God, then where else *can* you be yourself?'

A volunteer on Iona

Prayer

Think of those in history who had to 'live in the closet',
who couldn't be themselves in society …
Think of those who were found out,
or who dared to be themselves,
and suffered abuse, violence, death …

Think of gay, lesbian, bisexual and transgendered people
who must still live in the closet,
in fear of losing their jobs, their families, their friends;
in fear of being ridiculed, beaten up, killed ...

Think of women who have to act like men
in order to advance;
who have to become part of the old-boy network
in business, government, politics ...

Think of women in the Church who must still –
after 2000 years –
defer to men.

Jesus, you loved those on the margins and never judged people:
Help us to be more open, honest, accepting, loving.

On Easter morning you appeared to a woman
(because you knew the men would all be too scared or slow to get it)
and ordained her to go and tell the good news.

Jesus, some of us, men and women, are still too scared and slow.
Some of us still don't get it.
Christ, open eyes to the vision, gifts and skills of women;
transform your Church.
Amen

WATER

1 Kings 17:10
John 4:7–15

Water is essential for all dimensions of life. Over the past few decades, use of water has increased, and in many places water availability is falling to crisis levels. More than eighty countries, with forty percent of the world's population, are already facing water shortages, while by year 2020 the world's population will double. The costs of water infrastructure have risen dramatically. The quality of water in rivers and underground has deteriorated, due to pollution by waste and contaminants from cities, industry and agriculture. Ecosystems are being destroyed, sometimes permanently. Over one billion people lack safe water, and three billion lack sanitation; eighty per cent of infectious diseases are waterborne, killing millions of children each year.

World Bank Institute, Water Policy Reform Programme, November 1999

Prayer

O God, pour out on us the water of life that we may quench our thirst and draw our strength from you. Help us to stand alongside those who struggle daily for clean water so that all may be refreshed and renewed by your love. Amen

A prayer from Christian Aid

Action:

There are many traditional Christmastide rituals involving water: the Eastern tradition of the 'Solemn Blessing of the Water on the Feast of the Epiphany', the blessing of homes and doorways with holy water …

Pour a glass of water from your tap. Hold it up to the sunlight and look at it. Think about how amazing and precious it is; about how all life depends on water. Take a drink of delicious, cold water … Think about all the people in the world who don't even have a tap, who have to walk miles to a well (women usually). Think about those without clean water … without sanitation …

Water Aid
www.wateraid.org.uk

Christian Aid
www.christian-aid.org.uk

DOORWAYS

There was a tradition during Epiphany of blessing the home with holy water or with smoke/incense. There was a similar tradition of blessing doorways with 'blessed chalk'. On the doorway would be written the date of the new year, AD ____ +C+M+B: for Caspar, Melchior, Balthasar. This symbolised a commitment to welcoming Christ in the home throughout the year. This tradition is still popular in Latin America.

Matthew 7:13–14
Revelation 3:20

'Your door is open to all who call upon You.'

Rabia al-Basri, 8th-century Sufi poet

Prayer

I saw a stranger yesterday;
I put food in the eating place,
drink in the drinking place,
music in the listening place;
and in the sacred name of the Triune God
he blessed myself and my house,
my cattle and my dear ones,
for, as the lark says in her song:
'Often, Often, Often,
goes the Christ in a stranger's guise.'

Celtic rune of hospitality, **Iona Abbey Worship Book**

Action:

Bless the front door of your home, with holy water or blessed chalk or say a short prayer, and recommit to being open to welcoming Christ in the stranger's guise, in your home, in your heart.

Contributors

Helen Boothroyd is an Iona Community Associate and former member of the resident group at Iona Abbey. She now works as the Social Responsibility Development Officer for Churches Together in Cumbria, and also for the Ecumenical Council for Corporate Responsibility as the Church and Membership Relations Officer. She is co-author of *Holy Ground: Liturgies and worship resources for an engaged spirituality* (Wild Goose).

Ruth Burgess is a member of the Iona Community. She enjoys writing and sharing in participative liturgy, and editing liturgy resource books for Wild Goose Publications.

David Coleman and Zam Walker are URC ministers and members of the Iona Community. They are partners in ministry at Brighthelm URC in Brighton, parents to Taliesin and Melangell and staff to two cats. Their interests include body theology and digital art.

John Davies is a member of the Iona Community in Liverpool. He writes at www.johndavies.org

Leith Fisher has recently retired after ministries in Falkirk, Glasgow Calton and Welling-ton. Leith is a hymn writer and the author of *Will You Follow Me?: Exploring the Gospel of Mark* and *The Widening Road – from Bethlehem to Emmaus: An Exploration of the Gospel of Luke* (Scottish Christian Press).

Ian M. Fraser has been a pastor-labourer in heavy industry, a parish minister, Warden of Scottish Churches House, an Executive Secretary of the World Council of Churches, and Dean and Head of the Department of Mission at Selly Oak Colleges, Birmingham. He is the author of nineteen books, including *Strange Fire, The Way Ahead: Grown-up Christians*, and *Reinventing Theology* (www.ionabooks.com). Throughout his life Ian has travelled the globe, alone and with his wife, Margaret, visiting basic Christian communities. He is ninety years old.

Kathy Galloway is the current Leader of the Iona Community.

Tom Gordon has been chaplain with Marie Curie Cancer Care in their Edinburgh hospice for the past 14 years, having previously been a Church of Scotland minister in two Edinburgh parishes. He has been a member of the Iona Community since 1973, and is author of two books published by Wild Goose Publications: *A Need for Living* about his work in the hospice, and *New Journeys Now Begin* about issues of bereavement. He is married with three grown-up children and lives in East Lothian.

John Harvey is a minister member of the Iona Community, now retired. He was Warden of the Abbey and Leader of the Community, and served as minister in a number of parishes in Scotland.

Peter Millar is a well-known writer and an active campaigner for global justice. A member of the Iona Community, Peter and his late wife, Dorothy, lived in India for many years. Recently he has been active in the Wellspring Community in Australia. He lives in Edinburgh.

Neil Paynter has been an English teacher to immigrants to Canada, a nurse's aide, a night shelter worker, a 'counsellor', a community worker, a farm labourer, a fruit picker, a bookseller, a hospital cleaner, a stand-up comedian, a musician, an editorial assistant. He is an editor with Wild Goose Publications and the Editor of *Coracle*, the magazine of the Iona Community www.iona.org.uk

Jan Sutch Pickard is a writer and storyteller living on Mull, helping to lead worship in local churches. After working for the Community in Iona, she served with the Ecumenical Accompaniment Programme in Palestine and Israel, having been challenged to take a very different way.

Norman Shanks is a retired minister of the Church of Scotland who was Leader of the Iona Community from 1995 to 2002.

Thom M. Shuman is a poet/pastor in Cincinnati, Ohio. He is the author of *The Jesse Tree: Daily Readings for Advent* (Wild Goose Publications).

Alison Swinfen lives and works in Glasgow and is a member of the Iona Community. She is Professor of Languages and Intercultural Studies in the Faculty of Education at the University of Glasgow where she is Director of the Centre for Studies in Faith, Culture and Education.

Brian Woodcock is a previous Warden of Iona Abbey. He is the co-author of *Advent Readings from Iona* (Wild Goose Publications).

Footnotes

1. 'Voices raised in ancient songs …' – Lyrics from the song 'The Rest of the Year', from the album *Morning Glory*, Mary Travers, 1972.

2. 'Christmas Day … amazing God' prayer – by Ruth Burgess, from *Hay and Stardust: Resources for Christmas to Candlemas*, Ruth Burgess, Wild Goose Publications, 2005.

3. From *Jesus Means Freedom*, Ernst Käsemann, pp.151–2, SCM Press, 1969.

4. *Engaging the Powers*, Walter Wink, Fortress Press, 1992.

5. Ibid.

6. From *The Land: Place as Gift, Promise and Challenge in Biblical Faith* (2nd edition), Walter Brueggemann, Fortress Press, 2002.

Sources and acknowledgements

'Follow truth wherever you find it …' – George MacLeod, from an Advent talk, December 1958. From *Daily Readings with George MacLeod*, Ron Ferguson (ed.), Wild Goose Publications www.ionabooks.com

Scriptures quoted from *The New Revised Standard Version of the Bible*, copyright © 1989, Division of Christian Education of the National Council of Churches of Christ in the USA. Used by permission. All rights reserved.

Scriptures quoted from *The Good News Bible* published by The Bible Societies/Harper Collins Publishers Ltd., UK, © American Bible Society, 1966, 1971, 1976, 1992.

The Iona Community is:

- An ecumenical movement of men and women from different walks of life and different traditions in the Christian church
- Committed to the gospel of Jesus Christ, and to following where that leads, even into the unknown
- Engaged together, and with people of goodwill across the world, in acting, reflecting and praying for justice, peace and the integrity of creation
- Convinced that the inclusive community it seeks must be embodied in the community it practises

Together with its staff, the community is responsible for:

- The islands residential centres of Iona Abbey, the MacLeod Centre on Iona, and Camas Adventure Centre on the Ross of Mull

and in Glasgow:
- The administration of the Community
- Work with young people
- A publishing house, Wild Goose Publications
- Its association in the revitalising of worship with the Wild Goose Resource Group

The Iona Community was founded in Glasgow in 1938 by George MacLeod, minister, visionary and prophetic witness for peace, in the context of the poverty and despair of the Depression. Its original task of rebuilding the monastic ruins of Iona Abbey became a sign of hopeful rebuilding of community in Scotland and beyond. Today, it consists of about 280 Members, mostly in Britain, and 1500 Associate Members, with 1400 Friends worldwide. Together and apart, the community 'follows the light it has, and prays for more light'.

For information on the Iona Community contact:
The Iona Community, Fourth Floor, Savoy House,
140 Sauchiehall Street, Glasgow G2 3DH, UK.
Phone: 0141 332 6343
e-mail: admin@iona.org.uk; web: www.iona.org.uk

For enquiries about visiting Iona, please contact:
Iona Abbey, Isle of Iona, Argyll PA76 6SN, UK.
Phone: 01681 700404

For books, CDs & digital downloads published by Wild Goose Publications:
www.ionabooks.com